PRE-ARYAN TAMIL CULTURE

SALMON BOOKS

PRE-ARYAN TAMIL CULTURE

P T Srinivasa Aiyangar

SALMON BOOKS

Chennai New Delhi

SALMON BOOKS

ISBN 9789349032941 Salmon Books

Printed and bound in India No. 44, Nallathambi Street, Triplicane, Chennai 600 005

MJP 075

Publisher : C. Janarthanan

Publisher's Note

The legacy of a country is in its varied cultural heritage, historical literature, developments in the field of economy and science. The top nations in the world are competing in the field of science, economy and literature. This vast legacy has to be conserved and documented so that it can be bestowed to the future generation. The knowledge of this legacy is slowly getting perished in the present generation due to lack of documentation.

Keeping this in mind, the concern with retrospective acquiring of rare books has been accented recently by the burgeoning reprint industry. Salmon Books is gratified to retrieve the rare collections with a view to bring back those books that were land-marks in their time.

In this effort, a series of rare books would be republished under the banner, "Salmon Books". The books in the reprint series have been carefully selected for their contemporary usefulness as well as their historical importance within the intellectual. We re-construct the book with slight enhancements made for better pre-sentation, without affecting the contents of the original edition.

Most of the works selected for republishing covers a huge range of subjects, from history to anthropology. We believe this reprint edition will be a service to the numerous researchers and practitioners active in this fascinating field. We allow readers to experience the wonder of peering into a scholarly work of the highest order and seminal significance.

Salmon Books

Pre-Aryan Tamil Culture

BY

P. T. SRINIVASA IYENGAR, M.A.

(*Reader in Indian History, Madras University.*)

A LITTLE more than a year ago, on the invitation of the Syndicate of the Madras University I delivered the Sir S. Subrahmania Iyer lecture. I chose for the subject of that lecture the 'Stone Age in India' and gave an account of the life of the Indian people so far as it could be inferred from the relics of the Stone Age collected so far. Then I described that lecture as the first chapter of Indian History. My book on *Life in Ancient India in the Age of the Mantras*, published more than fifteen years ago, is the third chapter of the History of India. The lectures I am going to deliver now,[1] will constitute the second chapter of this entrancing story of the continuous evolution of Indian life from its start when man first appeared on this globe. The proper history of India is not the story of the rise and fall of royal dynasties, nor that of frequent invasions and constant wars, but that of the steady growth of the people in social, moral, and religious ideals, and their ceaseless attempts to realize them in actual life. Hence the work of the historian of India, as I understand it, is chiefly concerned with the construction of pictures of how the people, age by age, ate and drank, how they dressed and decorated themselves, how they lived and loved, how they sang and danced, and how they worshipped their gods and solved the mysteries of human existence.

THE SUBJECT

To the good old Vedic word 'Ārya', European scholars have attached varying connotations. A hundred years ago comparative philology was in its childhood and anthropology in an embryonic condition, and German Sanskritists invaded the realms of anthropology and imposed on it the theory that a highly civilized Aryan race, evolved in the central Asian Highlands, flowed down in various streams to India, Persia, Armenia, and the different countries of Europe, fertilized those countries and sowed the seeds of civilization far and wide. Soon this theory was modified by transferring the original centre of the Aryan race to Europe. The patriotism of French and of German scholars impelled them to rival with each other and to conclude that the motherland of each of them alone could support the honour of being the first centre of Aryan culture. Others assigned this honour to Scandinavia, to Finland, to Russia. As seven cities claimed Homer dead, so several countries claimed to be the original land of the Āryans. Then the Italian Anthropologists came into the scene and proved that the Āryans who invaded Greece, Rome and other European countries were savages who remained in the Stone Age when their neighbours had reached the Bronze Age and that wherever they settled

[1] A course of lectures delivered at the University.

in old times they destroyed the pre-existing civilization, for instance, in Crete and Etruria. To-day anthropologists say that all the races of the world are more or less mixed and that there never was a distinctive, pure Āryan race. The benefit of the theory of a conquering, civilizing Aryan race is now reserved only for Ancient Indian History, text-books of which teach that the Vedic culture was developed outside India and was imported into that country, ready made, by conquering invaders. But a careful study of the Vedas, such as is found in my *Life in Ancient India in the Age of the Mantras*, reveals the fact that Vedic culture is so redolent of the Indian soil and of the Indian atmosphere that the idea of the non-Indian origin of that culture is absurd. So we have got to restore, to the word 'Ārya', its original meaning found in the Vedas. The Rishis of the Vedas used the word 'Ārya' without any racial implications, but only in the sense of a people who followed the fire-cult as opposed to the fireless-cult. In the Vedic times two cults prevailed in India: (1) that followed by the Āryas to whom Sanskrit was the sacred tongue, the language of the Gods, who made offerings to the Gods through Agni, because they believed Agni to be the mouth of the Gods, and (2) that followed by the Dasyus whom the Āryas described as *anagni*, the fireless. Thus Arya was always in India a cult name, the name of a method of worship, whose main characteristic was the lighting of the sacred fire. There were two forms of the Ārya fire cult—the *Grihya* and the *Śrauta*, the cult of one fire and the cult of three fires, the *Ekāgni* and *Tretāgni*, the simple domestic fire-rites still performed in the houses chiefly of the Brahmanas and the gorgeous sacrifices, chiefly conducted by *Rajas* in ancient India up to the age of the Armageddon on the plains of Kurukshetra, and now almost extinct. The Ārya rites, besides being characterized by the mediation of the Fire-God, also required the use of Sanskrit *mantras*, which were promulgated by the ancient seers called Rishis; the Dasyu rites had no use for fire or for Sanskrit *mantras* or for a privileged class of expert priests.

When did the Ārya rites rise? It is impossible to determine when the concept of fire as the mouth of the Gods was worked out or when the cult of one-fire began. But it is possible to find out when the three-fire cult commenced. The Vedas and the Purāṇas assert that Purūravas first lighted the triple fire in Pratishṭhāna (now Prayāga or Allahabad); and though many royal dynasties rose and fell during the Age of the Rishis, we learn from Pargiter's *Studies of the Traditional History of Ancient India* that more than a hundred kings of one dynasty in particular reigned from the time of Purūravas down to the middle of the first millennium before the Christian era. Disregarding the Paurāṇika claim of incredibily long reigns for some of the kings of this dynasty and allowing a modest average of twenty-five years to each of them, we reach the very probable conclusion that the three-fire cult and the promulgation by the Rishis of the associated Vedic *mantras* on a large scale began about 3000 B.C. Now from the Vedic *mantras* we learn that there was intimate commercial intercourse, though there were cult rivalries, between Southern and Northern India, from the beginning of the age of the Rishis. South Indian articles like pearl, mother of pearl, scented woods, elephants, gold, the pea-fowl, etc., were used in the land of the Āryas (Āryāvartta); a very careful study of these Vedic *mantras* also reveals that the languages of South and

North India began to influence each other, however faintly, from the beginning of the Vedic Age. An analysis of the information contained in these *mantras* also discovers the fact that the Āryas and the Dasyus, though violently opposed to each other in the cults they followed, had attained to absolutely the same level of general culture; except in the matter of religion and literature, they lived the same kind of life; they ate the same food, wore the same kind of clothes, had the same amusements, the same customs, manners, etc., and followed the same methods of making love and war.

Is there any way of constructing a picture of the life of any Indian people before the rise of the Ārya cult 5,000 years ago? The Tamils were the most highly cultured of the people of India before the age of the Rishis and it is proposed here to investigate the culture which the ancient Tamils attained to in South India, before the gorgeous three-fire Ārya rites spread, and the associated Vedic literature was promulgated, in the valleys of the Sindhu and the Gaṅgā.

Three Lines of Evidence

There are three lines of evidence which can be utilized for constructing a picture of the life of the ancient Tamils before the rise of the Arya triple-fire cult in India, north of the Vindhyas. The first source of information regarding ancient South Indian life is the catalogue of prehistoric antiquities of South India, of artefacts, discovered by geologists and others, belonging to the Neolithic and early Iron Ages and deposited in the various museums of India. The study of these artefacts has to be supplemented by a careful examination of the sites whence these relics of ancient Indian man have been derived and which represent the settlements of Neolithic and early Iron Age men. Besides a careful study of ancient settlements the investigator ought also to observe the sites of ancient graveyards and conduct excavations ot Neolithic and early Iron Age graves in the Tamil country before he can understand their implications with regard to the lives led by the ancient Tamils. The second line of evidence is furnished by a study of the words which the Tamil language possessed before it came in any kind of contact with Sanskrit, the sacred language of the Āryas. Nouns and verbs constitute the trunk of a language and the objects and actions which nouns and verbs refer to must have been possessed by or known to the speakers of a language before they could use those essential parts of speech in their talk. If we could make up a list of the nouns and verbs which, we are certain, belonged to the earliest stratum of the language of a people, we may infer from it what objects they handled or had observed, what actions they were able to perform, in other words, what was the nature of the life that they lived, what was the general culture they had attained to. This is the main object of this study. Our third line of evidence is the early literature of the Tamil people. The existing specimens of this literature no doubt belong to times later than what we are investigating. But we are certain that the even tenor of the life of the people in that ancient epoch was not disturbed by catastrophic changes; therefore, as the life of the people mirrored in the early literature, which we now possess is, but an unbroken continuation of that of the earlier epoch, the evidence of that literature can be used to confirm the conclusions reached by the use of the other two lines of evidence. It is proposed in this study to construct a picture of the culture of Tamils five thousand years ago by utilizing these sources of information.

The Evening of the Lithic Epoch

An account of the life of the South Indians of very ancient times derived from a study of the artefacts of the stone ages has been given by me in my *Stone Age in India*. The life of the marauder, of the hunter and the worker in bamboo, of the cowherd and the shepherd, of the farmer and the weaver, and of the fisherman, the salt-scraper and the sailor, had all been evolved amongst them while yet in the New Stone Age, as is proved by the fact that they made polished stone tools necessary for the pursuits of the different means of livelihood associated with these forms of ancient culture. All these different pursuits existed at the same time, each in the region suited to it.

The life of the people at the end of the lithic times may yet be found in the interior of the Tamil land. There still exist in the heart of the Tamil country hamlets and villages where the ubiquitous Telugu Komaṭi is not found, where the ministrations of the all-pervasive Brāhmaṇa do not exist, and where even the *Kabandha* arm of British trade has not introduced kerosene oil and the safety match, called by the people *maṇṇeṇṇey*,[1] earth-oil and the fire-stick, *tīkkuchchi*,[2] where the whistle of the steam-engine and the toot of the motor horn has not yet been heard, and if you wipe off from the picture of the life of the people there the part played by iron tools, you can see with your eyes the slow placid life of the stone-age man exactly as it was in ten thousand B.C. Even in other parts of the country, which have participated in the elevation of culture due to the later discovery of iron, to the spread of the Ārya culture by the Brāhmaṇas, and to the development of internal trade during the long ages when there were numerous shufflings of dynasties of Indian Rajas and of foreign trade after European ships pierced the extensive sea-wall of Bhāratavarṣha, the greater part of the life of the people is but the life of the stone-age man, exactly as it was when Indian man was in the lithic epoch of culture.

The Dawn of the Iron Age

About seven thousand years ago, began the Iron Age in India. I assign a greater antiquity to the Iron Age in India than most scholars are inclined to admit, because the Vedic culture which began at least five thousand years ago was a culture of an advanced iron age. Prior to it flourished the cultures revealed by the excavations at Adichchanallūr in the Tinnevelly District and Moheñjo Daro and Harappa in the Indus valley. Moreover I shall presently prove that the Iron Age began when Tamil had not come in any kind of contact with Sanskrit

[1] மண்ணெண்ணெய். [2] தீக்குச்சி.

the linguistic vehicle of Vedic culture. Hence two thousand years before Pūrūravas lighted the triple-fire at Pratishṭhāna is not at all an exaggerated estimate of the length of the Pre-Vedic Iron Age in ancient India.

In India the Stone Age quietly passed into the Iron Age. In other parts of the world, the Stone Age was followed by the Copper Age, in which people made their tools (and ornaments) of copper and they discovered methods of hardening copper and made copper knives with edges as sharp as steel ones, an art which is now forgotten. The Copper Age was soon followed by the Bronze Age, in which they learnt to make an alloy of copper and tin, which was very much harder than copper. But in South India as in China, no brief Copper Age or long Bronze Age intervened between the Neolithic Age and that of Iron. 'Professor Growland, F.R.S., the great metallurgist and the successful explorer, archæologically, of the Japanese Islands, has expressed the idea that the smelting of iron may have been hit upon by accident while experiments were being made. This lucky accident may well have happened in India, where the iron industry is one of great antiquity (far greater indeed than in Europe, e.g., at Hallstat or Le Tené) and iron ores occur so largely.' [1] An examination of several Neolithic sites proves that the passage from the Lithic to the Iron Age was not catastrophic but that the two ages overlapped everywhere. Stone tools continued to be used long after Iron tools were made, more especially on ceremonial occasions, for the stone tool being the older one, was sacrosanct and alone possessed ceremonial purity, and hence stone tools occur along with iron ones in the graves of the early Iron Age.

Mr. Vincent A. Smith, the historian of India, an expert numismatist and not primarily an investigator of pre-historic antiquities and one totally ignorant of South Indian life or history and of early South Indian artefacts, assumes without a shadow of proof that iron was 'utilized in Northern India from at least 1000 B.C.', and that 'in Southern India the discovery or introduction of iron may have occurred much later and quite independently.'[2] Here are two gratuitous assumptions. The Vedic culture which was developed in India at least before 3000 B.C., was an Iron Age culture. The iron (*āyasī*) castles, mythological or actual, spoken of in the Vedic *mantras* and the distinct reference to *syāmamayas*,[3] black metal, are enough to prove this. So far as South India is concerned, Foote, who has examined most South Indian pre-historic sites so far known, has concluded that the antiquity of the iron industry of India is far greater than in Europe; and every one who has opened graves of the later Stone Age and the earlier Iron Age and studied the pottery associated with stone and iron tools and has also carefully examined settlements of those ancient times can easily satisfy himself that iron was discovered and worked in South India many millenniums before the beginnings of the Christian era. Soon after iron was discovered, South Indians learned to isolate from their ores gold, silver and copper and make ornaments and utensils of these metals. They also arrived at the general idea of metal as a material for household utensils in addition to stone and

[1] Foote, *Prehistoric Antiquities*, p. 25. [2] *Oxford History of India*, p. 4.
[3] *Atharva Veda*, xi. 3, 7.

wood previously used. They gave to metal the name of *pon*,[1] the lustrous material, from *pol* [2] to shine Gold was also called *pon*, the metal *par excellence*, as well as *tangam*,[3] the superior metal, *uyarnda pon*,[4] the superior (ever clean) metal. Iron was *irumbu*,[5] the dark metal, from *ir*,[6] dark (whence *iravu*,[7] *irā*,[8] night, *iruḷ*,[9] *iruṭṭu*,[10] *iruṭchi*,[11] darkness, *irundai*,[12] charcoal). Probably *irumu*[13] was the earlier form of Telugu *inumu*. Iron was also called *karumbon*,[14] meaning the black metal. Silver was *veḷḷi*,[15] the white metal, and copper *śembu*,[16] the red metal. That these four metals were alone known to ancient Tamil India and that tin, lead, and zinc were not known is proved by the fact that the Tamil names of these latter have been borrowed from Sanskrit. Thus tin is *tagaram*,[17] lead is *īyam*[18] (from Sanskrit *sīsam*, through Prakrit), and Zinc is *tuttam*[19] (whence the English word *tutty*, polishing powder) or *nāgam*.[20] Tin and lead are also respectively called *veḷḷīyam*,[21] and *kārīyam*,[22] white and black *īyam*,[23] under the mistaken idea that they were black and white varieties of the same metal. Brass, an alloy of copper and zinc, was also borrowed from Aryan India, its name *pittaḷai* [24] being borrowed from the Northern dialects. Bronze, an alloy of copper and tin, was not unknown in ancient Tamil India, for a few bronze implements and ornaments have been discovered in early Iron Age graves ; one such, a tiny *kūja* [25] (with its mouth so small that the little finger could not be squeezed into it). I recovered from an ancient grave, associated with a bill-hook, whose peculiar shape, similar to that of the weapon of the village gods, betokened its great age ; and this vessel was made of an alloy of copper and tin, which, on chemical analysis, was found to be remarkably free from impurities. The Bronze Age in Europe extended over long centuries ; but there was no necessity in South India for a Bronze Age, because the people had discovered iron before bronze and iron is a much better material for tools than bronze. The goldsmiths of India have used bronze only for polishing hammers and for stamps and dies, because these have to be made of a material both hard and incapable of being covered with rust, which would deteriorate the faces of polishing-hammers and destroy the delicate lines of the designs incorporated in stamps, dies, and moulds. Otherwise iron alone was the material used for tools in South India throughout the ages. Bronze was called in ancient Tamil *uṟai*,[26] but the fact that more bronze was imported from Northern India than was made in Southern India, is proved by the use of the words *kañjīyam*,[27] *kāñjiyam*,[28] from Sanskrit *kāmsyam*, and *tāram*,[29] from Sanskrit *tāra*, radiant, shining, as well as the artificial compound words *veṅgalam*,[30] the white vessel Malayalam *veḷḷōḍu*,[31] the white shell. Bronze was worked to some extent in South India, but 'the numerous bronze objects, many of which are of great beauty from the cemeteries of the South, do not belong to an age characterized by the sole use of that alloy.'[32]

[1] பொன். [2] பொல். [3] தங்கம். [4] உயர்ந்தபொன். [5] இரும்பு. [6] இர். [7] இரவு. [8] இரா. [9] இருள். [10] இருட்டு. [11] இருட்சி. [12] இருந்தை. [13] [illegible] [14] கரும்பொன். [15] வெள்ளி. [16] செம்பு. [17] தகரம். [18] ஈயம். [19] துத்தம். [20] நாகம். [21] வெள்ளீயம். [22] காரீயம். [23] ஈயம். [24] பித்தளை. [25] கூஜா. [26] உறை. [27] கஞ்சியம். [28] காஞ்சியம். [29] தாரம். [30] வெண்கலம். [31] வெள்ளோடு.

[32] J. Coggin Brown, *Cat. of Prehistoric Antiquities in the Indian Museum*, p. 8. As Foote, too, remarks, 'as it fell out, however, the discovery of the alloy [bronze] was not made in India till after the art of iron-smelting had been acquired and iron weapons and tools had come largely in use.' *Op. cit.*, p. 25.

The Copper Age in North India

There is some evidence that there was a copper age in some parts of Northern India, which preceded the iron age there. Implements composed of practically pure copper have been found at several sites in Northern India, chiefly in the Upper Ganges Valley. Besides, at Gungeriah in the Balaghat District of the Central Provinces has been found a hoard, which 'according to Sir John Evans . . . is the most important discovery of instruments of copper yet recorded in the old world. In 1870 no less than 424 hammered copper implements, made of practically pure metal, weighing collectively 829 pounds, and 102 thin silver plates were discovered there. The copper implements are extremely varied in form, principally consisting of flat celts of many different shapes. There are also many long crowbar-like instruments with an expanded lunette-shaped chisel edge at the lower end, which may be designated as 'bar-celts'. The silver objects are all laminæ about the thickness of ordinary paper, comprising two classes, viz., circular disks and 'bull's' heads. The Gungeria deposits although found south of the Narbada River, is clearly to be associated by reason of its contents with Northern India.'[1] The Upper Ganges Valley was the home of the Arya cult in ancient days. Hence copper became a holy metal in that cult; copper knives were used in some sacramental acts, e.g., marking cattle's ears,[2] hence copper vessels to Brahmanas even to-day possess ceremonial purity which bronze and iron vessels do not possess and are used for holding consecrated water during ceremonial worship. Not so outside the Arya cult, where copper is not considered holier than iron, for it was not discovered earlier than the black metal in South India.

Iron Age Antiquities

Tools of various shapes have been recovered from the graves of this period. From one site on the Shevaroys in the Salem District Foote got 'a large axe, a very fine bill-hook of large size with its handle in one piece, a sharp sword and two javelin heads made with tangs instead of sockets.'[3] From another site were got 'axe-heads, spear heads and fragments of blades of large knives or small swords. The iron axe-heads had a broad butt unlike a very good one (found in another place, which had) a very taper butt end expanding into a rather leaf-shaped blade. The method of fastening the iron axe-heads to their helves would seem to have been that adopted nowadays or certainly not very long ago, namely, of inserting the butt-end of the axe-head into a cleft in a piece of hard wood with a couple of rings and a wedge to tighten the hold of the helve. The rings are placed on either side of the butt end, and the wedge is driven tightly through the ring spaces and prevents the axe-head from slipping ; but the lower end also prevents the cleft in the helve from extending downwards.'[4] The shapes of the bill-hooks and some other tools of the

[1] J. Coggin Brown, *op. cit.* p. 10.
[2] *Lohita Svadhiti*, *Ath. Ved.*, vi. 141, 2.
[3] Foote, *op. cit.*, p. 62.
[4] *Ibid.*, p. 63.. Cf. the way in which the blades of spades, *maṇveṭṭi*, are furnished with handles now.

early Iron Age were exactly like those of the implements now in the hands of the village gods, as I found from a specimen obtained from a grave in the Pudukotta territory. While the shapes of tools used for secular purposes have changed with time on account of changes of fashion or other causes, the gods have stuck to the oldest fashions of tools.

Pre-historical iron tools have not been found in sufficiently large numbers considering the wide spread of iron manufacture in ancient India; for iron objects of all kinds are with great ease 'utterly destroyed and lost by oxidation when exposed to damp, yet, from the very durable character of the pottery the iron age people produced and the vast quantity of it they left, it is evident that in a large number of cases they must have occupied the old neolithic settlements; and the celts and other stone implements are now mixed up with the highly polished and brightly coloured sherds of the later-aged earthernware. Except in a very few cases the dull-coloured and rough surfaced truly (or rather early) neolithic sherds occur but very sparingly '.[1] Indian iron age pottery was so good that Foote remarks that the people who could make such high class pottery . . . must have attained a considerable degree of civilization.[2] Foote discovered at Maski near Raichur, in the Hyderabad State, 'the right jamb of the door of a small hut-urn, the prototype of the hut urns now met with in various parts of the country, some of which show remarkable resemblance to the same objects of Western classical antiquity, such as were found under the volcanic tufa near the Alban Lakes to the South of Rome. They were in some cases filled with the ashes of the dead after cremation, which were introduced by a little front door. The door was secured in place by means of a rope passing through two rings at its sides and tied round it. The whole resembled in shape a cottage with vaulted roof '.[3] The little door of another little hut-urn found by Foote 'had no hinges but was kept closed by two rude bolts working through flattish rings, on either side of the door, into a wider ring in the centre of it. . . . One in the British Museum . . . . is filled with the ashes of the dead, which were introduced by a little door. This door was secured by a cord passing through two rings at its sides and tied round the vase. The cover or roof is vaulted and apparently intended to represent the beams of a house or cottage. The exterior had been ornamented with a meander of white paint, traces of which remain. The ashes were placed inside a large, two-handled vase which protected them from the superincumbent mass. They have no glaze upon their surface but a polish produced by friction.' [4] But these hut-urns probably belonged to a late age, when on account of the influence of the fire-cult, cremation had been adopted in the place of the more ancient custom of burial.

[1] Foote, *op. cit.*, p. 24.
[2] *Ibid.*, p. 25.
'The true iron-age vessel (pottery) is distinguished by showing rich colours and highly polished surfaces with, in some cases, elaborate and artistic mouldings.' Foote, *op. cit.*, p. 25; but Indian artists even of the ancient days avoided painting human figures, such as were 'admirably done by the Greek vase painters'. (*Ibid.*, p. 34.) The early Indian had generally a prejudice against portrait-painting or reproducing the figures of kings on coins.

[3] Foote, *op. cit.*, p. 35. Not only urns but temples also were shaped like huts.

[4] Foote, *op cit.*, p. 35

After describing the specimens of pottery found on the left bank of the Cauvery at the ferry at Lakshmanapuram, six or seven miles above the Narsipur Sangam (in Mysore), Foote remarks, 'the people that made the Lakshmanapuram settlement must have been very advanced to have used so varied a set of crockery.'[1] On the French Rocks, not far from Mysore City, Foote found a chatty with the *swastika* emblem. In another place he found 'a perforated disc made out of a piece of dark brown pottery which has been well ground round its periphery and has had a hole equally well-drilled through its centre.'[2] Apparently it was a spindle whorl. East of the big tank at Srinivasapur in the Kolar Taluk, 'several acres of ground are covered with much comminuted earthenware lying in a thin layer. The prevailing colour of the sherds is red but entirely black occurs also and some specimens are brown and grey, but very few of the latter are met with. The vessels were polished, or smooth, or rough, and a great number of them richly decorated with impressed patterns of pinnate or bipinnate fronds combined with linear bands, raised or sunk. Others have fillets of dots or pitlets or trellis work painted on the sides. In hardly any case is a pattern produced in duplicate and there is also great variety in the shapes of the lips of the different vessels as well as in their sizes. The fragments are referable to a considerable number of distinct forms as *lotas*, vessels with spouts, vessels with three or four legs, *chattis*, melon-shaped bowls, wide-mouthed bowls, vases, necks and feet of vases, lids and stoppers various in shape, also pottery discs for playing games and perforated discs of uncertain purpose. Half a dozen pieces of broken bangles of chank shell occurred scattered about in the layer of potsherds.'[3]

Early Iron Age Graves

At Ādichchanallūr, two miles west of Srīvaikunṭam in the Tinnevelly District there is 'an inexhaustible field of archæological research of the most valuable description'.[4] The burial site here extends over a hundred acres of land. It is a long piece of high ground on the south bank of the Tāmraparṇi. The site, like all sepulchral sites, is higher than the surrounding country and is rocky or waste land unsuited for cultivation. 'About the centre of the ground some three feet of surface soil is composed of gravel, with decomposed quartz rock below. The rock has been hollowed out for the urns, with a separate cavity for each of them. In this burial ground the objects were found both inside and outside large urns of a pyriform shape. The urns were at an average distance of about six feet apart and at from three to twelve feet or more below the surface. Some were found placed over other ones. An idea of the deposits which exist in the whole area may thus be obtained, as an acre probably holds over a thousand urns. This is the most extensive and important pre-historic burial place as

[1] Foote, *op. cit.*, p. 72. [2] *Ibid.*, p. 73. [3] *Ibid.*, p. 75.

[4] All the quotations in this paragraph are from Rea's *Catalogue of the Prehistoric Antiquities* of the place.

yet known in Southern India.' In the graves have been found articles of gold, bronze and iron and pottery. Among them were diadems of gold of various sizes and oval shape. 'Some have a strip extending beyond the two extremities with a small hole for a wire or string at each end. They are thin plates ornamented with triangular and linear dotted design. Of iron, many implements were found (Mr. Rea's list of them numbers 3,940), always placed point downwards, as if they had been thrust into the surrounding earth by the attendant mourners. There are no implements or weapons in bronze, all articles in this metal being vessels of varied shape, personal ornaments such as rings, bangles and bracelets, or ornaments which have been attached to the bases and lids of vases, such as buffaloes with wide curved horns. The domestic animals represented in bronze are the buffalo, goat or sheep and cock; and the wild animals are the tiger, antelope and elephant. There are also representations of flying birds. There are sieves in bronze in the form of perforated cups fitted into small basins, the metal of these cups being extremely thin, and the basins only a little thicker. The perforations in the cup are in the form of dots arranged in a variety of designs, chiefly concentric circles around the bottom, and concentric semi-circles sometimes interlying around the rim.' There is no evidence of cremation at the place; this assures the great antiquity of the remains, for the custom of burning corpses spread in Southern India along with the Aryan cult from North India.

In the Pudukottah territory I have found rows of early iron age graves several miles long. The one near the village of Annavāśal, ten miles from Pudukottah, is the most notable of these burial sites. The graves are of oblong shape, each oblong consisting of a double square, the side of the square being two cubits in length. It is lined throughout with well-polished stone slabs and the two compartments are separated by another similar slab forming a wall between the two. In one of the squares was probably buried in an urn a chieftain or other ancient nobleman and in the other his wife. There is a circular hole in the middle of the slab separating the compartments, probably to allow the ghosts of the buried persons to communicate with each other. In a niche in the recess in each compartment, a stone lamp was placed which was probably lighted when the person was let into the grave. Inside the urns, as in the graves of the previous age, were placed the ornaments and implements of the dead person, and a tray full of foodstuff. The tools found in these graves are both of stone and iron, proving that the older stone tools continued to be used, more especially, for religious purposes.

A new fashion of tombs called megalithic, because they were built of big blocks of stone, was introduced in the end of the neolithic or the beginning of the iron age. Modern anthropologists are of opinion that the fashion began in the Nile Valley and spread in the wake of an ancient Egyptian sun cult. This shows that there was much intercourse, cultural and commercial, between ancient India and Egypt.

Mr. Longhurst gives the following description of a megalithic tomb he found in Gajjalakonda, in Kurnul District. 'The tomb consists of a large rectangular chamber about 10 feet in length, 5½ feet in width and 7 feet in depth with a small entrance passage on the south side, 4½ feet in length, 1½ feet in width, and 3 feet high. The sides and floor of the tomb and entrance passage are walled in and flagged with massive slabs of cut stone which are firmly imbedded in the ground in an upright position and help to carry the heavy slabs above forming the roof over the tomb.'[1]

The archæologists' spade has recently brought to light two early copper age settlements of the Sindhu Valley, of more than six thousand years ago,—those of Harappa and Moheñjo Daro. The chief difference between these and the South Indian iron age sites is that in these there are relics of houses built of brick. Brick was used in North India millenniums before it was used in South India, for here very hard wood fit for house-building wa available in large quantities till about a thousand years ago. The existence of these two seats of high civilization in the valley of Sindhu disproves conclusively the dream of Sanskrit scholars that Aryan immigrants with their wives and children and with their Lares and Penates, and a ready-made civilization, manufactured outside India, quietly occupied the Panjab about 3000 B.C. and, when these Aryan settlers appeared there, the original dwellers of the region vanished like the mist before the rising sun and let the foreign invaders people the Punjab with a pure Aryan race, possessing the Aryan nose and the Aryan cephalic index, as the current theory maintains. These finds also prove that, contrary to the opinion of Mr. J. Coggin Brown, in the neolithic as well as in the early metal age, there was a uniform degree of civilization attained throughout India. The advances to higher and higher civilization were as even as it was possible to be in a vast country like India.

Thus the evidence accumulated by the investigators of prehistoric antiquities of India proves that even before the spread of the Ārya fire-cult in Northern India, the people had reached a stage of culture indistinguishable from that which they occupy to-day except for the changes introduced by the cotton and metal manufatcures of Western Europe during the last hundred years. The rise of the Ārya fire-cult did not alter the stage of culture reached by the people, for we find from the study of the Vedic *mantras* that there was no 'difference of culture between the Ārya and the Dasyu; according to the Hymns composed for performing the Ārya rites, the Dasyus lived in 'cities'[2] and under kings the names of many of whom are mentioned. They possessed 'accumulated wealth'[3] in the form of cows, horses and chariots[4] which though kept in 'hundred-gated' cities[5] Indra seized and gave away to his worshippers, the Āryas.[6] The Dasyus were wealthy[7] and owned property 'in the plains and on the hills.'[8] They were 'adorned with their array of gold and jewels.'[9] They owned many castles.[10] The Dasyu demons and the Ārya gods alike lived in gold, silver and iron castles.[11] Indra overthrew for his worshipper, Divodāsa, frequently mentioned in the hymns, a hundred stone castles[12] of the Dasyus. Agni worshipped by the Ārya, gleaming in

[1] *Annual Report of the Archæological Dept., Southern Circle, Madras, for 1914-15*, p. 40.
[2] R. V. i. 53. 8; i. 103. 3. [3] R. V. viii. 40. 6. [4] R. V. ii. 15. 4.
[5] R. V. x. 99. 3 [6] R. V. i. 176. 4. [7] R. V. i. 33. 4.
[8] R. V. x 69. 6. [9] R. V. i. 33. 8. [10] R. V. i. 33. 13; viii. 17. 14.
[11] S.Y.S. vi. 23; A. V. v. 28. 9; R. V. ii. 20. 8. [12] R. V. iv. 30. 20.

front of him, tore and burnt the cities of the fireless Dasyus[1] Bṛhaspati broke the stone prisons in which they kept the cattle raided from the Āryas.[2] The Dasyus owned chariots and used them in war like the Āryas [3] and had the same weapons as the Aryas. The distinction indicated by 'Ārya' and 'Dasyu' was purely a difference of cult and not of race or culture.[4]

LINGUISTIC EVIDENCE

We now come to another fruitful source of information, the chief means of the study of the subject, i.e., 'pure Tamil words', those belonging to the earliest stratum of the Tamil language, those that were used by the Tamil people before they came in any kind of contact with the users of Sanskrit or with the cult associated with that language. The nouns and verbs belonging to this ancient stratum of the Tamil language indicate objects and actions with which the Tamil people were familiar in that ancient epoch. These 'pure' Tamil words are called *tanittamiḻ moḻigaḷ*,[5] words untouched by foreign influence; they were used by the Tamils to serve the needs of the culture which they had evolved for themselves before they were influenced by any other people in the world. This method of inferring the culture of a people from a study of the words peculiar to them was worked by Schräder, a generation ago, in his *Pre-Historic Antiquities of the Aryan People*; but Schräder's work suffered from three disabilities: (1) The baseless dream of a homogeneous Aryan race radiating in all directions from a central focus and carrying the torch of civilization to the countries of Western Asia and Europe, has dissolved in the light of Anthropological knowledge. (2) The people that carried the Indo-European dialects and imposed them in those countries have been proved to be a mixture of several tribes; moreover these dialects in their wanderings picked up so many words from other dialects that the words common to all the Indo-European dialects are few. (3) Even these few have undergone many phonetic changes; the laws governing these changes are being worked out so very slowly that many equations of the early scholars, e.g., that of Greek *Ouranos* with Indian *Varuna*, have become discredited by later research. On account of these reasons several conclusions of Schräder have had to be given up by later scholars. But the method of investigation pursued by Schräder is sound and can very well be applied to Tamil. This language, as its speakers have always claimed to be, is indigenous to South India, and grew there undisturbed by foreign languages till it reached a high stage of literary development. The Tamil race has been a homogeneous one since the Stone Age. The first few foreign students of the Tamil language indulged in a wild speculation that the Tamil language and its ancient speakers entered India from Central Asia, simply because a few Brahui words were found to appear to be allied to Tamil. This is far too slender a basis for concluding that Tamil was originally a non-Indian language. Scholars of two generations ago were fond of wantonly dragging

[1] R. V. vii. 5.3. [2] R. V. iv. 28.5; x. 67.3. [3] R. V. viii. 24.27; iii. 30.5; ii. 15.4.
[4] P. T. Srinivasa Iyengar, *Life in Ancient India in the Age of the Mantras*, p.12.
[5] தனித்தமிழ் மொழிகள்.

imaginary ancient races on the map of the world, as easily as pawns are moved on a chess-board, without regard for physiographic difficulties.[1] Moreover, they were ignorant of the fact that the extensive and well-developed Stone Age culture of ancient South India, enshrined in the earliest stratum of Tamil is ample proof that the Tamils inhabited South India from time immemorial.

Method of Investigation

It is the case with Tamil, as with most other languages, that there are two stages in the formation of words, an unconscious and a conscious one. When the science of comparative philology was born, about a hundred years ago, it was imagined that at first men invented and spoke only roots and, later, some of the roots became worn out into prefixes and suffixes, prepositions and postpositions, and a German philologist had the hardihood to write Aesop's Fables in an imaginary Indo-Germanic root-language, a kind of ghostly *Ursprache*, which never existed. The science of linguistics has got over this crude supposition. All students of language now recognize that it is as absurd to think that primitive man met in a solemn dumb conclave and invented a series of roots, as it is to assume with Rousseau, that the savage started gregarious life with a 'social contract'. The process of language-formation and language-growth is mostly unconscious; and if a number of words of allied meaning are also etymologically allied, if primitive man used the same stem for expressing ideas which were fundamentally identical, the process was more or less unconscious. Thus in Tamil, *var* is the common element of a series of words: *varappu*[2] meaning limit, border, wall, dike or ridge round a ploughed field to retain water; *varambu*,[3] dam, way, limit, rule; *vari*,[4] line, row; *varišai*,[5] order, regularity, row; *varichchal*,[6] dart, surgeon's probe, *varivaḍiveḻuttu*,[7] written-letter, *eḻuttu*,[8] letter, the ultimate unit of language, being conceived as existing in two forms, the spoken form and the written form,[9] *varivari*[10] (*taṇṇīrviṭṭān*),[11] *Asparagus racemosus*, a linear-leaved shrub, *varuḍal*,[12] stroking, thrumming a stringed (musical) instrument, *varai*,[13] measure, limit, shore, ridge, hill, the straight bamboo, write, draw, *varaivu*,[14] measure, limit, bound, separation. The implication of these facts is not that the

[1] As Mr. G. Elliot Smith has remarked (*vide Nature* January 1, 1927, p. 21) 'in ethnology emotion still counts for more than reason. The dominating principle is still to force the evidence into conformity with certain catch-phrases from which a long line of philosophers have been striving to rescue the study of mankind and make a real science of it.'

[2] வரப்பு. [3] வரம்பு. [4] வரி. [5] வரிசை. [6] வரிச்சல். [7] வரிவடிவெழுத்து. [8] எழுத்து.

[9] In this connection may be remembered Pavanandi's definition:

மொழிமுதற் காரண மாமணுத் திரளொலி யெழுத்து.

eḻuttu, the sound, formed by a group of atoms, which is the first cause of words *Nannūl*, 58. Eḻuttu has two manifest forms, the spoken and the written.

[10] வரிவரி. [11] தண்ணீர்விட்டான். [12] வருடல்.

[13] The word *varai*, வரை. appears in Telugu as *vrāyi*, by a process of oscillation of accent from the first syllable to the second syllable, of the consequent degeneration of the vowel of the first syllable, and the return of the accent to the new first syllable. This oscillation explains the formation from Tamil *uvan* of *vān*, *vāṇḍu*, *vāḍu*, from Tamil *maram* of *mrānu*, and hundreds of other similar formations.

[14] வரைவு.

South Indian man, when he was still dumb, arrived at the highly abstract concept of a limit marked by a straight line by a mysterious mental process unassisted by language, whereas modern man with his highly developed intelligence cannot engage himself in abstract thought without the help of words, that the primitive Tamil then invented the root *var* to express this concept, and later, formed the above words by ringing changes on the root. Language formation and linguistic growth and change are semiconscious or rather unconscious mental processes like the song of the lark or the gambol of the kid. It was when a people first came in intimate contact with a language other than their own and compared the two and noticed differences in the structure of words, of phrases and of sentences between the two languages, that they began to study their own language and the science of grammar was born. After such a contact with a foreign language, languages enter on a conscious stage of growth. Thus the words of a language belong to two stages of the growth of that language. (1) An early unconscious stage of word-invention, during the period when the language has not yet come into contact with a foreign language. Nouns belonging to this stage are called in Tamil grammar *iḍukuṟippeyar*,[1] symbol-names, names given to things as a mere mark, a symbol, for some reason not known. These words are the oldest words of any language. (2) A later conscious stage of word-making. Words belonging to this stage are compounds consciously invented by combining *iḍukuṟi* words of one's language into new combinations; thus, when the Tamils wanted a word for 'brick', which was used as a material for house-building only in a very late stage of South Indian history, that after contact with Sanskrit, they invented two compound words, (*a*) *śuḍumaṉ*,[2] burnt clay. (*b*) *śeṅgal*,[3] red stone. Of these, the first word did not appeal to the Tamil people and died an early death; the second has stuck on to the language. Similarly in our own days, we have invented compounds like *iruppuppādai*,[4] the railroad, *minsāram*,[5] electricity, etc. Such names are named by Tamil grammarians as *kāraṇappeyar*,[6] casual names, because the reason why the names were given to the objects is evident.[7] These two classes of names, *iḍukuṟippeyar* and *kāraṇappeyar* are called in Sanskrit *Rūḍhi* and *Yoga*, original and derived. Or the speakers of a language when they borrow a thing from a foreign people, may borrow also its foreign name and may partially or totally remould it in accordance with the phonetic framework of the mother-tongue. Thus the Tamils of an earlier epoch borrowed the Sanskrit word *ishṭikā*, brick, and turned into *ishṭigai*,[8] or *iṭṭigai*.[9] Often they absorbed the foreign word as it was, e.g., *āṇavam ::lam*,[10] *śashṭi*,[11] etc. The former are called by Sanskritists, *tadbhava*, and the latter *tatsama*. We, too, nowadays, get both *tadbhava* and *tatsama* words from English. Thus we speak of *tē*[12] and also *tea*, of *maistri* and *master*, etc.

[1] இடுகுறிப்பெயர். [2] சுடுமண். [3] செங்கல். [4] இருப்புப்பாதை. [5] மின்சாரம். [6] காரணப்பெயர்.

[7] Some Tamil grammarians make a further distinction between *kāraṇappeyar* and *kāraṇa iḍukuṟippeyar*; but this distinction does not affect the argument developed here and so need not be noticed. Others would regard verbs turned into names as *kāraṇappeyar*, e.g. *kal*, stone, from verb *kal*, to dig, etc., but this refinement, too, will not affect our argument, for the root is an *iḍukuṟi*.

[8] இஷ்டிகை. [10] ஆணவமல [illegible]

Of these two kinds of words, *iḍukuṟippeyar* and *kāraṇappeyar*, the first alone will serve the purpose of this enquiry. They alone come down from the far off ages when the Tamil language was born, when objects and actions were named unconsciously or semi-consciously.

Other words will not serve our purpose. Modern Tamil vocabulary includes words borrowed from English, French, Dutch, Portuguese, Persian, Arabic, Sanskrit and Prakrit. Of the loan-words from Sanskrit, some have been borrowed wantonly, i.e., when there are many Tamil words to express the ideas; this was partly due to Brāhmaṇas whose familiarity with Sanskrit made them import such words in their Tamil speech and writing. This extensive borrowing was also due to the necessities of rhyme and assonance, a great characteristic of Tamil poetry. Loan-words began to enter Tamil not before 1000 B.C. and cannot be of any use in investigating the life of the Tamils before they came into contact with other nationalities, except that words not wantonly borrowed may be used as negative evidence to show what the Tamils were not acquainted with before such borrowing. But the date of these borrowings cannot be fixed. So even this negative evidence is not of much use. Similarly what are called *kāraṇappeyar*, words deliberately invented to name things and express ideas for which there were no *iḍukuṟippeyar*, cannot also serve our purpose, for such casual names can be invented at any stage of a language and cannot be proved to have existed or to have not existed at any particular period of time.

Hence *iḍukuṟi* names alone will be used in this enquiry. Such words in Tamil are practically root-words, without the wrappings of prefixes, augments, suffixes, etc., which disguise the root in Sanskrit words and make Sanskrit etymology so difficult and in some cases unconvincing. As these *iḍukuṟi* words are naked root-words they belong to the earliest stage of Tamil, the stage when the language was unconsciously forged by the stone-age man. Examples of such words are *maṇ*,[1] *pul*,[2] *uṇ*,[3] *pō*,[4] *tī*,[5] *nīr*,[6] *mīn*,[7] *vān*,[8] *ā*,[9] *kā*,[10] etc. The stage of the invention of such simple root-words cannot occur more than once in the history of a language. First because it is a stage of unconscious development of a language; secondly, if roots could be invented at any stage of a language, there would be no necessity for loan-words and consciously invented compounds at all. When men after progressing beyond the earliest stage of a language found or made new things which required names, the native power of inventing roots having become exhausted, they semi-consciously extended the meanings of old words by the processes of metaphor and metonomy. Examples of words which belong to this stage are, *maṟai*,[11] shield, from *maṟai*, to hide, *pon*,[12] metal from *pol*,[13] to shine, *śembu*,[14] a pot from *śembu*, copper, itself from *śe*,[15] red. This may be treated as a second semi-conscious stage of the development of a language. These words are practically *iḍukuṟi* words, and will be utilized in this enquiry. A language becomes fully conscious only when it comes in contact with foreign languages; then it finds its soul, as it were, and becomes conscious of its structure; then alone it forges compound

[1] மண். [2] புல். [3] உண். [4] போ. [5] தீ. [6] நீர் [7] மீன். [8] வான். [9] ஆ;
[11] மறை [12] பொன். [13] பொல். [14] செம்பு. [15] செ.

causal names like *parimā*,[1] horse, the fast-going animal, *vaigalvaru-mīn*,[2] the morning star, words which will not serve the purpose of this investigation.

One more preliminary question has to be dealt with. With regard to most words now belonging to Tamil, the separation of pure Tamil words from those borrowed from Sanskrit is very easy. But most Sanskrit scholars assume that every Tamil word which looks like a Sanskrit one must have been borrowed from Sanskrit by the Tamils. When the speakers of two different languages come in touch with each other, the probabilities are that each language will borrow words from the other. Thus the names of articles produced only in South India, such as pearls, pepper, cardamoms, must certainly have been borrowed by Sanskrit from Tamil. Hence Sanskrit *maricha*, *muktā*, *ela*, are derived from Tamil *miriyal*[3] or *miḷagu*,[4] *muttu*,[5] *ēlam* ;[6] there are other Sanskrit words borrowed from Tamil wantonly which Sanskrit scholars wrongly claim to belong to Sanskrit, e.g., *nīram*, *mīnam*, evidently derived from Tamil *nīr*,[7] *mīn*,[8] for we cannot imagine that the Tamils were drinking water and eating fish for ages without names for these objects and deferred naming them till Sanskrit speakers presented them with names for them. Many such words can be ṛescued for Tamil from the hands of Sanskrit scholars , but in this enquiry for the purpose of disarming criticism, words which might be legitimately claimed to be Tamil, though they look like corresponding Sanskrit words, have not been much pressed into service.

Even after giving the benefit of the doubt to Sanskrit, it will be found that there is in Tamil a strikingly large variety of names for objects and actions. The wealth of synonyms for names of familiar objects will be found to be enormous as this investigation progresses. It looks as if when man began to invent words, he was in a state of childhood and as a child revels in the use of toys and is never tired of playing with them, primitive man used the power of inventing words as his great toy and invented a number of names for the same thing. Love of certain objects familiar to them may perhaps have been another motive for this multiplication of *iḍukuṛi* synonyms : but whatever it was, it is of use in this our enquiry into the conditions of life of the ancient Tamils.

Evidence of Literature

The third source of information for this study is early Tamil literature. The age to which this literature belongs has been the occasion for much dispute. The controversy has centred round a statement made at first by the commentator on *Iṛaiyanāragapporuḷ*[9] and repeated by later commentators. It is to the effect that there were three epochs of ancient Tamil Literature, each marked by the existence of a *Śaṅgam*,[10] academy of its own, presided over, each by the members of a particular dynasty of Pāṇḍya kings, whose capitals were respectively *Madurai*, swallowed long ago by the sea, *Kabāḍa-puram*[11] and *North Madurai*, i.e., the present city of that name.

[1] பரிமா. [2] வைகல்வருமீன். [3] மிரியல். [4] மிளகு. [5] முத்து. [6] ஏலம். [7] நீர். [8] மீன் [9] இறையனாரகப்பொருள். [10] சங்கம். [11] கபாடபுரம்.

This tradition says that the first *Śaṅgam* lived for 4,440 years, the second, for 3,700 years, and the third for 1,850 years. Much importance cannot be assigned to these precise figures, because early South Indian history does not reveal the existence of any particular era for the calculation of the passage of time in years from the year one of that era. Even eras established outside the Tamil country, like the Śālivāhana era, were adopted in South India not more than six hundred years ago. Dated lists of early Tamil kings do not, and cannot, on account of the want of an era, exist. The kings of these three dynasties are said to have been respectively 89, 59 and 49 ; this would give these Pāṇḍyas lengths of reign which no student of history can accept. The average length of the reigns of kings of dynasties which have lasted long, can range between twenty and thirty, but cannot mount up to fifty or sixty. Hence the alleged durations of the Śaṅgams are impossibly long and are also incapable of being checked by means of other sources of information, and useless as evidence of age. Moreover the commentator on *Iṛaiyanāragapporuḷ* who is our first informant about the three Śaṅgams is said to be Nakkīrar.[1] But the commentaries themselves name a series of ten scholars, beginning from Nakkīrar, each the pupil of his predecessor. The last of them, Muśiṛiyāśiriyar Nīlagaṇḍanār,[2] must therefore be the author of the commentaries as we now have them, though they may be claimed to possess a few sentences coming down from Nakkīrar's time. Moreover these commentaries embody a poem of 329 stanzas, whose hero is a Pāṇḍya king, Parāṅguśan Śaḍayan Māṛan Arikēśari,[3] who flourished about A.D. 750. Thus the earliest record about the chronology of the Saṅgams is found in a book composed in the latter half of the eighth century and cannot have much evidential value, specially as there was a total absence of contemporary chronological records before that age. Let us turn now to the internal evidence of early Tamil poems. One of these decidedly claims to belong to pre-Christian times. This is an ode of twenty-four irregular lines[4] sung by Murañjiyūr Muḍināgarāyar,[5] a poet of the first Śaṅgam of tradition, in honour of Sēramān Peruñjōṛṛu Udiyan Śēral Adan,[6] a Śēra king, and attributing to him the honour of feeding the armies of both sides in the Bhārata battle. Almost all modern enquirers agree that the middle of the first millennium B.C. was the epoch of the great war between the Kauravas and the Pāṇḍavas. There is no reason, except prejudice, to discredit the chronological claim of this ode. Hence we may conclude that from the beginning of the second millennium B.C., if not earlier, the kings of the three early Tamil royal houses, the Śēra, the Śōḷa and the Pāṇḍya, as well as several petty chiefs of South India, patronized minstrels called Pāṇar,[7] who, with the Yāḷ[8] on their shoulders, wandered from court to court and sang beautiful odes on the adventures of kings and nobles in love and war, or, as they called it, on *Agam*[9] and *Puṛam*.[10] Many of these odes are now lost, because they were preserved only in the archives of human memory ; but a great

[1] நக்கீரர். [2] முசிறியாசிரியர் நீலகண்டனார். [3] பராங்குசன் சடையன் மாறன் அரிகேசரி.

[4] *Puṛanānūṛu*, 2.

[5] முரஞ்சியூர் முடிநாகராயர். [6] சேரமான் பெருஞ்சோற்று உதியன் சேரல் ஆதன். [7] பாணர்.

[8] யாழ். [9] அகம். [10] புறம்.

number of them were collected in later times into anthologies called *Agaṉānūṟu*,[1] *Puṟanāṉūṟu*,[2] *Naṟṟiṇai*,[3] *Kuṟundogai*,[4] etc. These poems, though their vocabulary shows a very slight admixture of Sanskrit and Prakrit words, due to the intercourse of South India with North India ever since the beginning of the Vedic Age, notwithstanding the rivalries between the fire cult of the latter with the fireless cults of the former, are yet entirely free from the influence of Sanskrit literature in the subject matter of poetry and in literary form. These poems undoubtedly reflect the conditions of life peculiar to the ages when they were composed. Unlike the artificial epics of post-Christian Sanskrit literature, these early Tamil poems, which it is now usual to call *Śaṅgachcheyyuḷ*[5] are a mirror of the ages when the poets lived. Catastrophic changes occur in the life of a nation only when there is a violent contact with foreign people of a different stage of culture. As no such event occurred in South India, it is certain that the life-conditions reflected in these old poems are at least partial echoes of those of the previous far off ages which we are now discussing. But at the same time it must be remembered that the evidence of this literature should be pressed into service very cautiously, when we are sure that the customs and manners referred to therein are not later developments but evidently come down from early times.

Besides these anthologies there exists the wonderful grammar called *Tolkāppiyam*,[6] one book of which, called *Poruḷadigāram*,[7] is the grammar of ancient Tamil poetry. This book belongs to the period when Ārya influence had fully penetrated South India; it was composed by *Tṛnadhūmāgni*, a Brāhmaṇa of the Kāppiya (Kāvya) clan, a branch of the Bhārgava Gotra, members of which began to migrate into South India under the leadership of Paraśurāma when he retired from North India after his quarrels with the sons of Arjuna Kārttavīrya (about 2500 B.C.). Tolkāppiyar studied pre-existing grammars written by several previous Tamil *Pulavar*[8] (scholars), and then composed the *Tolkāppiyam*. But wherever possible he tries to impose the Ārya canon law on the Tamils and to equate Tamil customs, social and literary, to Ārya ones; yet his attempts to mix up Arya and Tamil culture is not much of a success, for the two cultures, one based on the fire cult and the other on the fireless cult, one, the product of a religious aristocracy and the other, of a social democracy, could blend as little as oil and water.

Hence it is easy to separate the Tamil culture embodied in ancient Tamil poetry and in the *Poruḷadigāram* from the well-known Ārya culture of the Ārya law-books first imported into Tamil country by the early Brāhmaṇa settlers. From these several sources of information it is possible to construct a picture of the life which the Tamil people led from the later Stone Epoch onwards in the ages that may be called Pre-Aryan, of the life that they led and the culture they had evolved independently of any other people, till the large incursions of the Jainas, the Buddhas and the Brāhmaṇas in the first millennium before Christ caused the final blending of the Ārya culture and the

1 அகநானூறு. 2 புறநானூறு. 3 நற்றிணை. 4 குறுந்தொகை.
5 சங்கச்செய்யுள். 6 தொல்காப்பியம். 7 பொருளதிகாரம். 8 புலவர்.

Tamil culture and the present, mingled culture of South India started on its glorious evolution.

Combining these two sources of information, the pure Tamil *iḍukuṛi* words coming down from the early ages and the evidence of early Tamil literature, it is proposed to make further rents in the veil which time has woven round the life led by the Tamils five thousand years ago.

Social Organization

The ancient Tamil people noted that the surface of the habitable portions of the earth could be divided into five natural regions, which they called *Pālai*[1] or sandy desert land, *Kuṛinji*,[2] mountainous country, *Mullai*,[3] forest tracts, *Marudam*,[4] the lower river valley, fit for agricultural operations, and *Neydal*,[5] the littoral region. They noticed that in each region was evolved a different kind of human culture. In *Pālai* grew the nomad stage, in *Kuṛinji*, the hunter stage, in *Mullai* the pastoral stage, in *Marudam* the agricultural stage, and in *Neydal*, the fishing and sailing stage, of human development. Not only were these different stages of human culture evolved in these different regions, but each stage continued to exist in its own region, after other stages grew in theirs. The men of these regions were respectively called *Maṛavar*,[6] *Kuṛavar*,[7] *Āyar*,[8] *Uḻavar*,[9] and *Paradavar*.[10] The recognition of the different kinds of life led by these five different classes of men is a wonderful anticipation, made several millenniums ago, of the very modern science of Anthropogeography. This science is the rival of Ethnology. The latter claims to be able to divide men into races with varying permanant physical and mental characteristics, flowing from microscopical bodies called chromosomes which pass from parent to offspring. Notwithstanding heroic efforts for a hundred years to calculate the cephalic index and the co-efficient of racial likeness, ethnologists have not been able to hit on any characteristic, unchangeable mark of race. Anthropogeography, on the other hand, holds that what are called racial characteristics are the result of the action of the environment within which a people grow, which is called the area of characterization of a race. It is remarkable the Tamils reached this idea in remote ages and defined the five natural regions, and classified races as five, each of whom followed professions suited to the region inhabited by them. Besides this horizontal classification, there was a vertical classification of the people of any one region into *Mannar*,[11] kings, *Vaḷḷal*,[12] petty chiefs, noblemen, *Veḷḷāḷar*,[13] owners of fields, *Vaṇigar*,[14] merchants, all of whom were called *Uyarndōr* [15]or *Mēlōr*,[16] the higher classes, and *Vinaivalar*,[17]and *Aḍiyōr*,[18] the working classes and personal servants.[19] This second classification is solely based on the standing of people in society, and is one that has evolved everywhere in the world. On these two classifications, the Brāhmaṇas who carried the Arya cult into Southern India in the first millennium before the Christian era, imposed a third

[1]பாலை. [2]குறிஞ்சி. [3]முல்லை [4]மருதம். [5]நெய்தல். [6]மறவர். [7]குறவர். [8]ஆயர். [9]உழவர். [10]பரதவர். [11]மன்னர். [12]வள்ளல். [13]வெள்ளாளர். [14]வணிகர். [15]உயர்ந்தோர். [16]மேலோர். [17]வினைவலர். [18]அடியோர்.

[19]Tolkāppiyam, *Poruḷadigāram*, i. 21-32.

one, the socio-religious division of the people into four Varṇas. This division arose on account of the necessities of the Vedic fire-cult. This cult evolved into a vast system of rites which were celebrated during long periods of time, the Sattra Yāgas occupying twelve to a hundred years, and required the growth of the Brāhmaṇa Varṇa, consisting of men who from childhood memorized the immense literature of the Vedas and subsidiary works, the Śruti and the Smṛti, and were trained in the correct performances of the complicated Arya rites and, being experts in the religio-magical ceremonies, acquired a high standing in society. Then there were the Kings of several grades, Chakravarttī, Mahāraja, Rājā, who with their blood-relatives formed the Kshattriya Varṇa, and whose function it was to protect the people and the fire-rite from being oppressed by enemies. For the special benefit of the Kshattriyas, the more gorgeous fire-rites, such as Rājasūya, Abiṣheka, Vājapeya, Aśvamedha, etc., were evolved. The bulk of the people were the Vaiśyas (from *viṣ*, people) devoted to the ordinary pursuits of man—agriculture, trade and the tending of cattle. The Vaiśyas had the privilege of paying for and deriving the benefits accruing from the minor yāgas which the Brāhmaṇas performed on their behalf. The last Varṇa included the serving classes, called Śūdras. This fourfold classification is neither regional nor racial, neither social nor professional but one correlated entirely to the fire-rite. When the Brāhmaṇas settled in Southern India and the ancient Tamil Rajas desiring to secure the benefit of the Yāgas, accorded to the fire-priests a supreme position in society, the Brāhmaṇas naturally tried to introduce their socio-religious organization into Tamil society. But a religious oligarchy and a social democracy could not very well mix with each other. Hence the Brāhmaṇas did not succeed in arranging the people of Southern India as members of the four varṇas as they did in North India. The Rajas who actually ruled in the provinces of peninsular India were given the privileges of Kshattriyas with regard to the fire-rites—that of paying for them and deriving the invisible (*adṛṣhṭa* or *apūrva*) effects of the Yajña and were even admitted to the Bhāradvāja Gotra ; but the scheme of four varṇas necessary to a people, every detail of whose daily life, from urination to cremation, was influenced by the fire-rite, could not well spread among the Tamils, whose life for many millenniums previously was mainly secular and based on social democracy and among whom the Arya fire-rite, as it had lost its vitality before the Brāhmaṇas migrated to Southern India, did not spread. It only led to the confusion of caste and the prevalence of social jealousies that have characterized the life of South India for a thousand five-hundred years; for, we learn from the *Tēvāram*,[1] of Tirunāvukkaraśu Nāyanār,[2] that there was in his day, as there is to-day, a consciousness of rivalry, if not jealousy, between the Brahmins and the non-Brahmins or, as they were then called, *Ariyan*,[3] and *Tamiḻan*.[4] The cause of this was

[1] தேவாரம். [2] திருநாவுக்கரசுநாயனார். [3] ஆரியன்.

[4] தமிழன். ஆரியன் கண்டாய் தமிழன் கண்டாய்.
Tirumaṛaikkāḍu Tiruttāṇḍagam, 5.
செந்தமிழோடு ஆரியனைச் சீரியானை.
Tiruvāvaḍuduṛai Tiruttāṇḍugam, 10.
ஆரியந் தமிழோ டிசையானவன்.
Tirukkaḍambanduṛai Tirukkuṛundogai, 3.

as follows: The Brāhmaṇas obtained in India north of the Vindhyas, i.e., Āryāvartta, a premier position in society on account of their being the hereditary depository of secular and religious lore, and of being expert in priestly duties and in wielding the words of power (mantras) which almost coerced the gods to grant gifts to those who solicited them. But the Kshattriyas who were quite as learned as the Brāhmaṇas and besides, had the prestige of the royal varṇa, and the Vaiśyas, who were rich burghers and wielded much political influence, acted as a check on the expansion of the privileges of the Brāhmaṇas. In South India, however, the Brāhmaṇas added to the intellectual qualifications they already possessed—scholarship in Tamil literature and ability to compose Tamil poetry.[1] Moreover, there was no true Kshttriya or Vaiśya Varṇa in South India. Though according to the *Bhagavad Gītā*[2] agticulture, tending cattle and commerce were the legitimate occupations of the Vaiśyas, the Brāhmanas did not extend the Vaiśya status to the Tamils that pursued these avocations in the *Mullai* and *Marudam* regions and did not admit them to the benefits of the fire-rite, even of the domestic variety, which was open to the three higher varṇas. On the contrary they invented for them pseudo-fire-rites, usually called Purāṇoktam ceremonies, as opposed to Vedōktam rites. An example of this is the addition of circumambulating the fire, *Tīvalañjeydal,*[3] to the ancient marriage ritual of the Tamils, to make it look like the genuine Arya wedding-rite. At the same time the worship of Śiva and Vishṇu in temples, which was evolved from pre-vedic forms of worship and is described in the Agamas, whose vital characteristic is Bhakti, and not Jñāna such as the Vedānta Sutras teach, spread in the Tamil land, because Bhakti which neglects the Varṇa classification appealed to the democratic instincts which got the upper hand after the decay of the fire-rite. Hence the Ārya classification of four varṇas never really spread in South India and Tolkāppiyar who laboured hard to equate the several classes of Tamil society to the varṇas of the Āryas carefully avoids the use of the word Śūdra as referring to any section of the Tamils. This brief sketch of the history of Ārya ideals in South India explains to a large extent the prevalence of the conflict of caste in the present time.

THE FIVE CLASSES: THEIR MODES OF LIFE AND RELIGIOUS PRACTICES

In my Stone Age in India has been given a very brief account of the life of the five classes of people in the five regions. A more extensive account will be given here. In the *Pālai* lived the *Kaḷḷar*[4] and the *Maṛavar*,[5] nomad tribes of adventurous warriors; as the soil of the region where they dwelt was infertile and totally unproductive, they lived by preying upon the wealth accumulated by the dwellers of other regions. They sacrificed animals and, at times, men too, to the dreaded local god or goddess; these deities have been, in comparatively recent times, idealized and turned into aspects or subordinates

[1] As illustrations Kapilar, Paraṇar, and the Saint-child Tirujñāna Sambarda Nāyanār may be mentioned.

[2] *Bhagavad Gītā*, chapter xviii. 44. [3] தீவலஞ்செய்தல். [4] கள்ளர். [5] மறவர்.

of the world-mother, *Kāḷi*[1] or of her husband, *Śivan*.[2] Many of their sacrificial stones, called in early times *Kandaḷi*,[3] have become the objects of worship in shrines which have grown around them. They also planted stones in memory of the heroism of their dead heroes exhibited in wars or on other occaions, and worshipped the stones.[4]

The clubs with which Stone Age men dealt death to their human and animal foes and the bill-hooks with which the later Iron Age men cut up those animals, as well as images of tools cut on stones are still in many shrines the only physical representatives of the gods they worshipped and can to-day be seen not only in *Pālai* land but also in all other parts of the country. In later days there were migrations of men and cults from region to region; the various tribes coalesced with each other by marriage and other causes; hence the practices of *Pālai* are now observable in the four other regions too.

Ancient worship was inseparably associated with ritual dance. The dance which constituted the worship of *Koṟṟavai*, the goddess of victory, is elaborately described in canto xii of *Śilappadigāram*, called *Veṭṭuvavari*.[5] This description contains the later, much developed ritual, but from it one or two ancient factors of the ritual dance can be extracted: 'The priestess who uttered the oracles of *Koṟṟavai*,[6] called Śālini,[7] was born in the family of *Maṟavar*, who bear in their arms a bow. In the high street in the middle of the village which was surrounded by a hedge of thorns and where the hunters ate their food jointly, she danced, being possessed by the goddess, the hair of her body standing on end. She lifted up her arms, and her feet kept time so well that the men wondered at the sight'.[8] And she uttered

[3] கந்தழி. This word literally means pillar, being a derivative of கந்து, post, and அழி, straw and therefore probably meant a pillar to which the sacrificial victim was bound with ropes of straw. In later times when nobler conceptions of the deity were reached கந்தழி was explained as the supreme substance, the Being above all elements of matter.

[4] They were called கந்தக்கடவுள். *Puṟam* 263 refers to the worship of the memorial stone of a man who stayed a hill-torrent like a dam. Numerous odes celebrate the memorial stones of warriors who died in battle. *Puṟam* 264 says that the stone was decorated with garlands of red flowers and peacock feathers and the hero's name was engraved thereon.

மரல்வகுந்து தொடுத்த செம்பூங் கண்ணியொ
டணிமயிற் பீலி சூட்டிப் பெயர்பொறித்
தினிநட் டனரே கல்லும்.

Agam 67 says that besides the above a board with a spear fixed on it was placed near and his other implements were also planted near the memorial.

நல்லமர்க் கடந்த நாணுடை மறவர்
பெயரும் பீடு மெழுதி யதர்தொறும்
பீலி சூட்டிய பிறங்குநிலை நடுகல்
வேலூன்று பலகை வேற்றுமுனை.

Excavations at Moheñjo Daro and Harappa reveal that writing was known in India five thousand years ago; hence it is not surprising to learn that the names and deeds of heroes were incised on stone in early days.

[5] வேட்டுவவரி [6] கொற்றவை. [7] சாலினி.

[8] வழங்குவிற் றடக்கை மறக்குடித் தாயத்துப்
பழங்கட னுற்ற முழங்குவாய்ச் சாலினி
தெய்வ முற்று மெய்ம்மயிர் நிறுத்துக்
கையெடுத் தோச்சிக் கானவர் வியப்ப
விடுமுள் வேலி யெயினர்கூட் டுண்ணு
நடுவூர் மன்றத் தடிபெயர்த் தாடி.

Lines 6–11.

warnings about the disasters that would overtake the villages for not having paid thei dues to the goddess. In the mountainous country, called *Kuṛiñji* lived the *Kuṛavar*, famous in later literature as the heroes of romantic love at first sight ; they led the semi-nomad life of the hunter ; they hunted with the bow and the arrow and fought wild animals with the *Vel.*[1] They cut up and skinned the animals they hunted and wore the untanned hide as their dress. They were also brave warriors.

Their women in the earliest days were clad in nothing but the atmosphere around or in hides or in *Maravuri,*[2] tree-flay, or in leaf-garments, called in Tamil, *taḻai-uḍai.*[3] Hence arose the custom of presenting a garment made of leaves and flowers to the bride as a symbol of marriage, as in Malabar to-day presenting a Muṇḍu,[4] short piece of cloth, to the bride is still the chief incident of the wedding-rite.[5]

These women wove baskets and made many other articles with the strips of the bamboo, occupations still followed by *Kuṛavar* throughout Southern India. Their favourite god was *Murugan,*[6] the God of the Hills, who has throughout the ages remained essentially a god enshrined on hill-tops, notwithstanding later affiliations with post-Vedic mythology. As Lord of the Hills, the abode of serpents, he reveals himself even to-day to his devotees in the form of a serpent. The hill country being at all times the home of romantic love at first sight, he was, and continues to be to-day, the boy-lover, the *Śēyōn,*[7]

[1] வேல். [2] மரவுரி. [3] தழையுடை. [4] முண்டு.

[5] The following are a few of the references to the practice of the presentation of a leaf-garment, *taḻai uḍai* in the early literature.

தீநீர்ப் பெருங்குண்டு சுனைப்பூத்த குவளைக்
கூம்பவிழ் முழுநெறி புரள்வரு மல்குல்.

Puṛam. 116.

The lap from which is dangling the leaf-garment made of the whole blossom of the water-lily which grows in deep springs of sweet water with its sepals open.

அளிய தாமே சிறுவெள் ளாம்ப
லிளைய மாகத் தழையா யினவே
இனியே பெருவளக் கொழுநன் மாய்ந்தெனப் பொழுதுமறந்
தின்னா வைக லுண்ணு
மல்லிப் படூஉம் புல்லா யினவே.

Ib. 248.

May it be blessed ! the little, white water-lily, when I was young, served for a leaf-garment ; now, when my excellent husband is dead, the hour of meals is changed, it provides me with my food during the melancholy mornings.

குன்றநாட
னுடுக்குந் தழைதந் தனனே யவையா
முடுப்பின் யாயஞ் சுதுமே கொடுப்பிற்
கேளுடைக் கேடஞ் சுதுமே.

Naṟṟiṇai. 359.

The hill-chief gave me a leaf-garment ; if I wear it, I am afraid I cannot satisfactorily answer the questions my mother will ask me about it ; if I return it to him I am afraid it will cause him pain.

சாரற்
றழையணி மருங்குன் மகளிர். *Kuṛundogai.*

The hill-women who wear a leaf-garment at their waist.

The wearers of this garment can still be seen in the hill-regions.

[6] முருகன். [7] சேயோன்.

the ever-youthful. When in later ages asceticism came to be a much respected way of life, and ascetics resorted to hills for peaceful meditation, he also became the ascetic god. Coming down from ages when man had not yet invented clothes, he is in many of his manifestations a naked god. Worship of the gods was in ancient days inseparably associated with ritual dancing, as is still the case with primitive people all over the world; and the ancient worship of Murugan was the dance called *Veṛiyāḍal*[1] or *Vēlanāḍal*,[2] performed by his priest, who, like his god, was called, *Vēlan*,[3] for both of them carried the weapon of the hill region, the *Vēl*, a spear, which in the stone age had a stone spear head and, on the discovery of iron, had a head made of that metal.[+]

The worship of Murugan included the offering of cooked rice and meat for the removal of ills caused by that god. 'O!' old vēlan, intoxicated with the spirit of Murugan! control the anger and help us. I beg one favour of you. If you offer along with many-coloured boiled rice the meat of a red sheep specially killed for the purpose, after marking her forehead (with its blood), will the god of the hill high as the sky who wears a garland eat the *bali* (and be pleased)?

In later times when religion in India developed noble concepts, attained giddy heights of supreme devotion and breathed the soul-satisfying atmosphere of philosophical insight, highly advanced associations

[1] வெறியாடல்.

முருகயர்ந்து வந்த முதுவாய் வேலன்
சினவ லோம்புமதி வினவுவ துடையேன்
பல்வே றுருவிற் சில்லவிழ் மடையொடு
சிறுமறி கொன்றிவ ணறுநுதல் நீவி
வணங்கினை கொடுத்தி யாயி னணங்கிய
விண்டோய் மாமலைச் சிலம்ப
னொண்டா ரகலமு முண்ணுமோ பலியே.

Kuṛundogai 362.

[2] வேலனாடல். [3] வேல

[+] This is a brief description of *Veṛiyāḍal* is from *Maduraikkāñji*. ll. 611–617.

அருங்கடி வேலன் முருகொடு வளைஇ
யரிக்கூ டின்னியங் கறங்கநேர் நிறுத்துக்
கார்மலர்க் குறிஞ்சி சூடிக் கடம்பின்
சீர்மிகு நெடுவேட் பேணித் தழூஉப்பிணையூஉ
மன்றுதொறு நின்ற குரவை சேரிதொறு
முரையும் பாட்டு மாட்டும் விரைஇ
வேறுவே றுகம்பலை வெறிகொள்பு மயங்கி.

The terrible *Vēlan* proclaimed the might of Murugan and danced around the people; the sweet-sounding musical instruments sounded in unison; they wore the *Kāñji* (காஞ்சி) flower—*Lawsonia spinosa*—which blossoms in the rainy season, and fixing in their hearts the image of the *Vēl* (வேல்) the lord, who shines with the beautiful *Kaḍambu* (கடம்பு) flower—*Eugenia racemosa*—embraced one another and caught hold of one another's hands and danced the *Kuravai* (குரவை) dance on the open fields; all through the village they hymned his greatness, they sang songs in his honour, they danced many dances and the blending of these sounds caused confusion.

The Vēlan proclaiming the might of Murugan refers to an ancient ceremony. When a man is in distress he consults the priest of Murugan, who throws about the seeds of the *Kaḻangu* (கழங்கு) or *Kaḻarkoḍi* (கழற்கொடி) *Guilandina bonduce*, and from the lay of the seeds on a plate reads the occult cause of the man's trouble and prescribes the worship of Murugan as a remedy. This ceremony is technically called *Kaḻangu*.

were woven round this and other gods of very ancient times, but yet numerous relics of South Indian religious life of ten thousand years ago are inextricably bound up with the worship of these gods to-day and these indicate the simple, ancient concepts and beliefs and customs of the Tamils of those far off days.

In the wooded tracts called *Mullai*, lived the *Iḍaiyar*, the men of the middle region, that lies between the uplands and the plains below. They were also called *Ayar* and *Kōnār*,[1] literally cowboys. They led a merry pastoral life tending cattle and playing on the flute, *kuḻal*, made of the bamboo, or of the stem of the water-lily, or of the cassia fruit or of the creeper jasmine. Besides playing on the flute, they spent their ample leisure in love-making in the forests which afforded ample cover for their amatory proceedings. The god of the *mullai* region was *māyōn*,[2] the dark-hued wonder-working *kaṇṇan*.[3] Their old women sprinkled the paddy from a *nāḻi*,[4] tubular corn-measure, along with sweet-smelling *mullai* flowers so that the bees swarmed round and sounded like the *yāḻ* and then bowed to their god.[5] Accompanied by children and relatives the crows ate the white balls of cooked rice along with fried *karunai*,[6] tuber which has dark eyes offered to the God.[7]

The worship of *māyōn* was also associated with innumerable religious dances, which can be observed to-day in cowherd villages when the annual festival in honour of this deity is celebrated. These dances were called *kuḍam*[8] or *māyōnāḍal*.[9] In Vedic times, Kṛṣhṇa, the Sanskrit form of the name Kaṇṇan, was a god or as the Rig-veda called him a demon, opposed to Indra. In the Purāṇas, too, there are evidences of an ancient Kṛṣhṇa cult opposed to the Indra-cult of the early Rishis.[10] In still later times Kaṇṇan became Kṛṣhṇa Paramātma, the fullest human manifestation (*Avatāra*) of Iśvara to the Indian people and has everywhere extinguished the worship of Indra. The legends regarding the boyhood life of Kṛṣhṇa have certainly come down from the ancient pastoral stage of human evolution, though not then localized in the forest of Brindāvanam. The bulk of cowherds to-day act out many of these legends and keep up the ancient pastoral dances of Kṛṣhṇa worship, but are absolutely untouched by the grand philosophical ideas which have gathered round the personality of Kṛṣhṇa. I therefore hold that the ancient god of the pastoral tribes evolved into Kṛṣhṇa and not that Kṛṣhṇa of the *Bhagavad Gita* deteriorated into a pastoral god in recent times.

The current theory about Kṛṣhṇa-worship is that the historical

[1] கோனார். [2] மாயோன். [3] கண்ணன். [4] நாழி.

[5] யாழிசை யினவண் டார்ப்ப நெல்லொடு
நாழி கொண்ட நறுவீ முல்லை
யரும்பவி ழலரி தூஉய்க் கைதொழுது
பெருமுது பெண்டிர். *Mullaippāṭṭu* 8-11.

[6] கருனை.

[7] பிள்ளை தழீஇக் கிளை பயிர்ந்து
கருங்கட் கருனைச் செந்நெல் வெண்சோறு
சூருடைப் பலி. *Naṟṟinai* 367.

[8] குடம். [9] மாயோனாடல்.

[10] This subject is fully discussed in my *Life in Ancient India*, pp. 131–2 and *Stone Age in India*, pp. 50–51.

person of that name, whose boyhood was spent in the pastoral country round Brindāvanam and who, later, as the king of Dvārakā, played a great part in the war of the Mahābhārata, was deified and after his death, the Krishṇa cult spread throughout India. In opposition to this theory I hold that the cult of Kṛshṇa, the boy-cowherd, comes down from the early pastoral stage of Indian life; it is impossible to believe that the later worship of Krishṇa, associated with the study of his *Bhagavad Gītā*, than which no grander philosophic work has been published to the world, spread to only one caste of South India—the cowherd caste—and became a cult of primitive ritual song and dance. It is much more reasonable to conclude that the primitive song and dance and merry-making which is the Kṛshṇa-worship of the cowherds is directly descended from the rites of very ancient pastoral times. The name *Kaṇṇan* is supposed to be derived from Prākrit *Kaṇha*, itself a degenerate form of Kṛshṇa. This kind of etymology is opposed to the fundamental principles of linguistic science, for it makes the absurd assumption that the literary dialect of a language precedes the common spoken dialect, whereas the spoken dialect must have existed for thousands of years before the literary dialect was developed.

To proceed from *Mullai* to *Marudam*; in the lowermost reaches of the rivers lived the farmers, of whom there were two classes, (1) the *Veḷḷāḷar*,[1] the controllers of the flood, who irrigated their fields when the rivers were in flood, and raised the rice-crop on damp rice-fields with the extraordinary patience and industry which only the Indian peasant is capable of; (2) the *Kārāḷar*,[2] controllers of the rain, who looked up to the sky for watering their fields, who stored the rain water in tanks and ponds and dug wells and lifted the water by means of water-lifts of different kinds, *ēṟṟam*,[3] *kabilai*,[4] *piḻā*,[5] *iḍā*,[6] and raised the millets, the pulses and other legumes, which along with the rice of the river valleys and the milk and the milk products (tyre and butter-milk and ghi, *tayir*,[7] *mōr*,[8] and *ney*[9]) of the *Mullai* region, form, even according to the latest scientific teaching, a perfect food for man containing the muscle-building, heat-generating, and vitamine requisites of a perfect dietary. The *Veḷḷāḷar* lived in the *Marudam* region, the river-valleys and just outside it lived the *Kārāḷar*. Beyond these regions where foodstuffs were raised, existed the black cotton-soil developed from the detritus of trap-rock charged with decaying vegetation, and fit for retaining moisture for a long time, and hence suited for the growth of cotton. Here cotton was raised and cotton cloth was woven; Indian people of the Stone Age possessed an abundance of cotton cloth, as weaving implements of stone testify, when the rest of the world was either sparsely clad in hides, or woven linen or wool, or revelled in primitive nakedness. Hundreds of finds of Neolithic tools required for these industries of the lower river valleys testify to their great development in these regions. These industries of the plains required the subsidiary one of woodwork. The people lived in wood-built houses; their granaries were made of wood; they used wooden carts, not different in build from the creaking ones now used for transport and numerous household utensils made of wood like tubs, mortars, pestles, etc.; and all the tools now used by the

[1] வெள்ளாளர். [2] காராளர். [3] ஏற்றம். [4] கபிலை. [5] பிழா. [6] இடா. [7] தயிர். [8] மோர். [9] நெய்.

village carpenter, but made of stone, as well as tools for stone-work, have been picked up from neolithic settlements. The chief god of the low country was the cloud-compelling lord of the atmosphere, who, as Indra, became also the chief recipient of the offerings made in the Vedic fire-sacrifices throughout North India; but in South India Indiran was the god only of the ploughland. Besides he was worshipped by the people with the fireless rites detested by the Āryas. Here 'he was the God residing in the land where, with toddy and garlands as offerings, the straight-horned and hanging eared goat is led to him'.[1] In Āryan India Indra was but the most prominent of the many gods worshipped by Brāhmaṇa priests, for their own benefit and the benefit of others, by means of fire-rites in sacrificial halls specially built for the purpose, Rājas and Vaiśyas having but the privilege of paying for the rites without officiating at them; but in South India Indiran was the sole god of the *Marudam* region and his worship was conducted without fire-rites and in it participated men of all castes and occupations, even men of the lower classes who would not be admitted even for menial service in *yajña śālās* and women of all ranks. Indra worship in South India was accompanied by merry-making and love-making of all kinds. Moreover the festival of Indiran was specially associated with lovers' quarrels and reconciliations, *ūḍal*[2] and *kūḍal*[3] and with special varieties of dancing. The modern Pongal feast is a relic of the harvest-festival associated with Indiran, as the name *bōgi paṇḍigai*,[4] Indiran-feast shows,[5] bōgi being a name of Indiran.

So great is the prejudice in favour of the North Indian origin of everything connected with religion that to claim the Indiran of *Marudam* as a Tamil God independent of the Indra of the Āryas is sure to raise as violent a burst of opposition as Indra's own burst of the thunder-cloud. To support the claim here made I offer the following considerations: (1) The people of the *marudam* regions of South India must have had an atmospheric god from about the end of the old Stone Age when they learnt to till the ground and sow seeds for raising foodstuffs, for their existence depended on such a god manifesting himself in the hot weather and striking the clouds with his thunderbolt so as to pour the life-giving rain on their thirsty fields. (2) To deny them an Indiran of their own would be to say that they had from time inmemorial another god of the same functions till about 2,000 years ago, when they borrowed the name of the chief God of the Ārya fire-rite, and that, after that fire-rite had almost become extinguished in Āryāvartta and after Indra had been superseded in popular estimation by Siva, Vishṇu, and Ambā. One is tempted to vary the joke about the author of the *Iliad*, that it was not composed by Homer but by another poet of the same name, and say that

[1] கள்ளுங் கண்ணியுங் கையுறையாக
நிலைக்கோட்டு வெள்ளை நாள்செவிக் கிடாஅய்
நிலைத்துறைக் கடவுள். *Agam*, 156.

[2] ஊடல். [3] கூடல். [4] போகிபண்டிகை.

[5] The utter difference between Indra-worship in North India and the இந்திர விழவு of South India can be realized by a study of canto v of *Śilappadigāram* இந்திர விழவு ஊரெடுத்த காதை, which is too long to be quoted here.

the Stone Age Tamils did not worship Indiran but another God of the same name and the same functions. The theory becomes more absurd if, with European scholars, it is held that Indra the God *par excellence* of the monsoon area was at first the God of the non-monsoon tracts outside India, that he was then taken into Northern India by Aryan emigrants and lastly, after a few thousand years' stay there, he leisurely migrated to the *marudam* region of Tamil India, where he was being worshipped by the people for many thousand years, previously by some name unknown, which name was suddenly extirpated without a trace by the newly imported name. (3) The South Indian Indiran-cult was in every one of its details and practices utterly different from the Vedic Indra-cult as pointed out above. (4) If South India borrowed Indiran from the Āryas, there is no reason why he should have his jurisdiction suddenly contracted and why he should be confined to the *marudam* region and should not have extended to all regions as it did in India north of the Vindhyas. On the contrary when the Arya concepts spread in South India along with the migration of Brāhmaṇas to the south of the Vindhyas, the functions of the Aryan Indra were added on to the Indiran of the Tamils, who was thenceafter called *Vēndan*,[1] King of the Gods. It is more reasonable to consider that the Indiran of the *marudam* became also the King of the Gods after the contact of the Tamils with the Āryas than that the extent of his empire was diminished by his invasion of South India. (5) If South India borrowed Indiran from North India, there is no conceivable reason why the ploughmen alone should borrow the God and not the people of other regions, such as *neydal* and *mullai*. (6) The South Indian worship of Indiran was not conducted by an expert caste as in North India. It is inconceivable that as soon as the Brāhmaṇas brought the Indra-cult to South India, they resigned their priestly functions with regard to this deity and his worship became a popular institution in which all castes and both sexes could take part. The Brāhmaṇa-rites and the old Tamil rites have not become mixed up though Brāhmaṇas have wielded supreme religious power in South India for 2,000 years, and though the two have co-existed for 2,000 years. Is it not then absurd to hold that at one moment in the past Indra-rites of North India became inextricably blended with Tamil rites. (7) The worship in each of the five regions consisted primarily in ritual dancing, peculiar to each region. This was accompanied by the singing of tunes, *paṇ*, special to each tract. There was also a special form of *yāḻ* for each natural region on which the tunes of that regions were played. In such worship. all people, whatever their status, took part, whereas in northern India, even during the performance of royal *yajñas*, such as *Rājasūyam*, Kings could not enter the *yajña śālā* except on one solitary occasion when they were temporarily invested with the rank of a Brāhmaṇa and allowed to make one *āhuti*, offering, in the fire nearest to the gate of the sacrificial hall. How the worship in which the Brāhmaṇa oligarchy alone could officiate could suddenly become a democratic institution it is impossible to conceive. (8) Convincing etymologies of the names of the Gods Krishṇa, Indra, and Varuṇa

[1] வேந்தன்.

from Sanskrit roots have not been found by scholars notwithstanding three thousand years of unexampled ingenuity. Hence there is no linguistic reason to claim that these names originally belonged to the Sanskrit language. (9) The possibility of North India borrowing names of objects and even of Gods from South India has not been investigated at all. There was plenty of intercourse between the people North and South of the Vindhyas in the remote ages. Therefore there is nothing to disprove the notion that the same Gods were worshipped throughout India even before the fire-cult rose to great popularity five thousand years ago. Hence the most probable conclusion is that when the Rishis moulded the Vedic cult they utilized the pre-existing gods and adapted them to their philosophical concepts. Such is what has taken place all over the world in the evolution of religion. Moreover it is only in recent times that the idea rose that Sanskrit, being a perfect language, could not have borrowed names from any other language. The ancient thinkers had no such illusion. *Mīmāmsā Sutras* I. iii. 9, says, *chodītam tu pratiyeta avirodhāt pramāṇena.* This implies that words borrowed from the *mlechchha* languages and used in the Veda ought to be understood in the sense they have in those *mlechchha* languages and not to be ascribed new meanings based on the *nirukta* or etymological speculations. Śabara gives as illustrations of such borrowing *tāmara*, lotus, *pika*, cuckoo, both Tamil words. I offer the suggestion that many more words were borrowed by Sanskrit from Tamil. Not as a proved conclusion, but merely to challenge enquiry I suggest that the word, so essential to later Sanskrit philosophy, *Māyā*, was coined from a Tamil root-word.

Māyā is a word which occurs in the Vedic *mantras*; there it does not possess the meaning of *Mūlaprakṛiti*, chaotic matter, that which is not *sat*, nor *asat*. In the *mantras* it merely means the wonder-working power exhibited by Indra and other gods. Gradually *Māyā* came to be specially associated with Vishṇu; in the *Bhagavad Gītā*, Kṛishṇa, the incarnate Vishṇu, speaks of *mama māyā duratyayā*, 'my Māyā difficult to transcend.' So Māyā came to mean the power, the magic might wielded by the Supreme Vishṇu in creating, and sustaining the universe and this is still the meaning of Māyā in Vaishṇava tradition. In the Śaiva schools Māyā became the wife of Śiva, the mighty mother of the universe, being Īśvara's power embodied in manifested matter. In the Advaita schools, she became identified with *Prakṛiti*, matter, which is a reality to embodied beings and vanishes without leaving a trace behind before the vision of him who has seen the light of Ātmā. Hence Advaitīs explain it by the jingle *yā mā sā māyā*, who is not, she is *māyā*; this ingenious and impossible derivation could have been invented only, after that incomparable philosopher, Śaṅkarāchārya, definitely and finally connected the word with that which exists as a phenomenon but does not exist as a noumenon. The older meaning of the word, from which this meaning has arisen, was wonder, astonishment, power of magic, cannot be derived from any Sanskrit root; but Tamil possesses a root that exactly suits the word and that is *māy*, [1] to be astonished, to vanish from sight. I am sure that on a careful study conducted according to the fundamental principles of modern etymological science, many Sanskrit words will be found to be borrowed from those of the languages which prevailed in India in the early Iron Age. At any rate the idea that the gods who were worshipped before the rise to popularity of the Ārya cult were borrowed and ennobled and idealized by the Rishis is not quite so absurd as people imagine.

Now Indra has become extinct in the *marudam* region. Ever since the worship of Siva and Vishṇu rose to mighty proportions from the sixth century A.D. onwards, under the inspiration of the singers of the Śaiva *Tevāram* and Vaishṇava *Pirabandam*, Indra disappeared. His place of popularity in the minds of the common people, especially of the river-valleys, has been usurped by a non-vedic God, who has no Tamil name but whose worship is most wide-spread in the Tamil country, viz., *Gaṇeśa* or *Vishvaksēna*, the generalissimo and the remover of difficulties. How this came about I cannot at all explain. I can only note in passing that while Indra was a constant rider on elephants, Gaṇeṣa combines in his person human and elephantine features.

From *marudam* I shall now turn to *Neydal*, the littoral region. Here were evolved the occupations of fishing, salt-scraping, salt-manufacture, and the selling of salt, of fresh fish and salted fish; they made canoes, dug-outs and wicker work boats; the *Paradavar* men sailed on the sea, at first hugging the coast, and, later, boldly struck across the black sea, *Karuṅgaḍal*,[1] and reached far off countries where they exchanged the cotton cloth and timber of South India for scented gums, sugar and other products of foreign lands. Their God was Varuṇan, another deity also invoked in the Ārya rites; but the worship of Varuṇan by the *Valaiñar*,[2] the men who plied the net, the lowest of the low, was of course very different from the fire-worship of the same deity. 'It is the new moon and the red-haired *Paradavar*[3] men have not gone along to fish in the broad, black, cold sea; with their dark-skinned women clad in green-leaf garments, in the midst of their huts, which were built on the sea-beach whose sands smell of fish and which had low roofs on which were placed the long angling rods, on the sands of the front yard on which the nets were spread like a patch of darkness on a moon lit-floor, they planted the horn of the gravid sword-fish and invoked on it their God. They wore (round their neck) garlands made of the cool flowers of the white *Kūdāḷam*[4] (a kind of *Solanum*), which grows at the foot of the *Tāḻai*[5] (screw-pine), and (on their heads) the flowers of the *tāḻai*, which has long petals; they drank the toddy from the palmyra which has a rough skin, and also the liquor brewed from rice, and danced. In the noisy part of *Pugār*,[6] where appearing like a red cloud on a black hill, and like a (red-haired) child at the mother's (black) breast, the Kāviri mixes with the clear and dark waters of the ocean-wave, they bathed to get rid of their sins, and, then, bathed in the river to get rid of the salt on their skins; they hunted for crabs and played in the spreading waves; they made

[1] கருங்கடல். [2] வலைஞர். [3] பரதவர். [4] கூதாளம். [5] தாழை. [6] புகார்.

images; they were intoxicated with the pleasures enjoyed through many senses and played with undiminished joy throughout the day.[1]

After reading this description of Varuṇa-worship it would be foolhardy to derive it from the Vedic Yajña, in which Varuṇa, Indra and Mitra were invoked.

KINGS

The institution of kingship was an ancient one among the Tamils, for several old words exist which mean a king: e.g., *Kōn*,[2] *Ēndal*,[3] *Vēndan*,[4] *Mannan*,[5] *Kuriśil*,[6] *Iṟaivan*;[7] besides, the words *Vaḷḷal*,[8] and *Aṇṇal*,[9] restricted in later usage to nobles or petty chiefs, rulers of small territories, *Kuṟunilamannar*,[10] but applied to kings also. The government of a people by a king was called *Āṭchi*,[11] an abstract noun from the verb *Āḷ*,[12] to rule over, from the noun *Āḷ*,[13] a subject, originally a person. Government was conceived as being similar to a herdsman ruling a herd, helping it to feed and protecting it from enemies. The name *Ēndal*,[14] (and *Vēndan*,[15] which perhaps is etymologically the same word) is derived from *Ēndu*,[16] to support, and refers to the chief function of a king, that of protecting his subjects from harm. But the oldest Tamil word for a king is *Kō*,[17] or *Kōn*,[18] which also means a cowherd. This implies that kingship arose first in the pastoral stage of the evolution of human life. It is in this stage that men began to acquire wealth, cattle, *paśu*,[19] *pecu*, being the earliest form of wealth that man could acquire. Pastoral life required that a tribe should settle with its wealth of cattle on a patch of grass-land. Unlike other forms of wealth, cattle and sheep constantly reproduce their kind, and herds always grow in size. The sons of a herdsman may partition the herd belonging to the family among themselves, but the pasture-land cannot thus be partitioned,

1 நெடுந்தூண்டிலிற் காழ்சேர்த்திய
குறுங்கூரைக் குடிநாப்பண்
ணிலவடைந்த விருள்போல
வலையுணங்கு மணன்முன்றில்
வீழ்த்தாழைத் தாட்டாழ்ந்த
வெண்கூதாளத்துத் தண்பூங் கோதையர்
சினைச்சுறவின் கோடுநட்டு
மனைச்சேர்த்திய வல்லணங்கினான்
மடற்றாழை மலர்மலைந்தும்
பிணர்ப்பெண்ணைப் பிழிமாந்தியும்
புன்றலை யிரும்பரதவர்
பைந்தழைமா மகளிரொடு
பாயிரும் பனிக்கடல் வேட்டஞ் செல்ல
துவவுமடிந் துண்டாடியும்
புலவுமணற் பூங்கானன்
மாமலை யணைந்த கொண்மூப் போலவுந்
தாய்முலை தழுவிய குழவி போலவுந்
தேறுநீர்ப் புணரியோ டியாறுதலை மணக்கு
மலியோதத் தொலிகூடற்
றீதுநீங்கக் கடலாடியு
மாசுபோகப் புனல்படிந்து
மலவ னாட்டியு முரவுத்திரை யுழக்கியும்
பாவை சூழ்ந்தும் பல்பொறி மருண்டு
மகலாக் காதலொடு பகல்விளையாடி.

Puttinappālai, 80, 104.

2 கோன். 3 ஏந்தல். 4 வேந்தன். 5 மன்னன். 6 குரிசில். 7 இறைவன். 8 வள்ளல். 9 அண்ணல். 10 குறுநிலமன்னர். 11 ஆட்சி. 12 ஆள். 13 ஆள். 14 ஏந்தல். 15 வேந்தன். 16 ஏந்து. 17 கோ. 18 கோன். 19 பசு.

for, where a small holding of a rice-field may well be cultivated by its owner and arable land may continue to be sub-divided into little plots for generations, pasture-land cannot thus be subdivided, for grass-fields below a minimum size are unfit for pasturing a herd. Hence the joint-family system became a necessity. The patriarch of a tribe thus acquired great influence and became its king. Hence the word *Kō*, cowherd, came to be applied to a king when kingship evolved.

The house where the king resided was the *Kōṭṭai*.[1] As the royal power increased, as the science of warfare developed, the royal residence, *Kōṭṭai*, became a fort. The fort was surrounded by strong walls, *araṇ*;[2] hence the fort was called *araṇmanai*;[3] *araṇ*[4] originally meant both beauty and defence, and hence came to be applied to the walls of a fortress, also called *madil*.[5] These walls were made of mud, mixed with boiled ragi flour and were so strong and elastic that they could resist battering very much better than inelastic brick or stone walls. In the Tinnevelly district there exists even to-day many a *madil* made after the ancient recipe, which are very difficult to pull down. The fort was surrounded by an *agaḷ*,[6] *agappā*,[7] or *agaḻi*,[8] a moat, (from *ag*[9], to dig, whence the following Tamil words are derived, *Agam*[10] home, inside, mind, the inner life, love, etc., *Agakkāḻ*,[11] heart-wood, *agaḍu*,[12] inside, *agaṇi*,[13] interior, heart-wood, also a rice-field dug out of the soil, *agappu*,[14] depth, *agalam*,[15] breadth, *agal*,[16] a bowl, *agavai*,[17] internal quality, *agal*,[18] to dig), *agappai*,[19] a ladle scooped out. The *agaḻ* was also called *uḍu*,[20] *ōḍai*,[21] *kayam*,[22] *kēṇi*,[23] *parigam*,[24] *parigai*,[25] *puriśai*[26] and *pāmburi*,[27] (that which surrounds a fort as closely as the skin round a snake). The wealth of names for the moat shows that it was a very familiar object to the ancient Tamils. The entrance to the fort was called *Koṭṭi*[28] and the batter, i.e., receding slope from the ground upwards behind a wall, topped by a flat platform, *Kottaḷam*.[29] *Ñāyil*[30] is the name of another part of a fortification: what it means is not known clearly. Within the royal residence there were many rooms, each called *aṟai*,[31] (from *aṟu*,[32] to cut off), a portion of the house walled off from other portions for special purposes. One of these rooms was the store-room, *Koṭṭaṟai*,[33] or *Koṭṭaḍi*,[34] (whence perhaps was derived the Sanskrit word *Koshṭa*). The state-room was the *Koluvaṟai*[35] or *Koluchchāvaḍi*,[36] where the king sat in state on occasions of ceremonial. This was called *koluviruttal*,[37] or *Vīṟṟiruttal*.[38] The *Koluchchāvaḍi* was no doubt decorated with flags[39] (*koḍi*,[40] *tugil*,[41] *togai*,[42] *śatti*,[43] *kattigai*,[44] *kadali*,[45] on these occasions, as well as with flowers and bunting, flowers and leaves playing a large part in South Indian life as will be shown later. On such formal occasions, the king wore a crown. As the crown was called *muḍi*,[46] band, we may be sure that it was a band

[1] கோட்டை. Another early word for a palace was *Kōil*, (கோயில்) which, after the rise of the grand modern temples, became restricted to Gods' houses.

[2] அரண். [3] அரண்மனை. [4] அரண் [5] மதில். [6] அகல். [7] அகப்பா. [8] அகழி. [9] அக். [10] அகம். [11] அகக்காழ். [12] அகடு [13] [14] அகப்பு. [15] அகலம். [16] அகல். [17] அகவை. [18] அகல். [19] அ [20] உடு [21] ஓடை [22] கயம். [23] கேணி. [24] பரிகம். [25] பரிகை. [26] புரிசை. [27] பாம்புரி. [28] கொட்டி. [29] கொத்தளம். [30] ஞாயில். [31] அறை. [32] அறு. [33] கொட்டறை. [34] கொட்டடி. [35] கொலுவறை. [36] கொலுச்சாவடி. [37] கொலுவிருத்தல். [38] வீற்றிருத்தல். [39] Flags used to decorate a street were called *viḍaṅgam* (விடங்கம்). [40] கொடி. [41] துகில். [42] தொகை [43] சத்தி. [44] கத்திகை. [45] கதலி. [46] முடி

of gold tied around the forehead, like the gold bands found at Ādichchana''ūr. Indian crowns of recent ages were tall conical caps of solid gold, imbedded with gems such as now adorn gods when going out on processions ; these are so heavy that gods alone can wear them for any length of time, and could not have been worn by the ancient Tamil kings, all the more so as kings, like all other men of the ancient Tamil country, grew a whole head of hair. Shaving was unknown in South India and was introduced by the Āryas ; this is proved by the fact that there is no proper, ancient Tamil name for the barber, and there are only words derived from the Sanskrit, like *pariyāri*,[1] *ambaṭṭan*,[2] *nāvidan*,[3] *maṅgali*[4] or descriptive compounds like *mayirvinaiyāḷan*[5] (hair-dresser), *māśutīrppōn*,[6] (one who puts an end to a hairy check). Moreover, throughout the interior of South India, people who have not taken to Aryan or European customs do not even now patronize barbers.

Wearing a crown and gold bracelets round the wrist, above the elbow and the ankles, (*Kaḻal*)[7] furnished with tinkling bells, (*śadaṅgai*),[8] garlands of pearls, *muttu*,[9] coral, *pavaḷam*,[10] and rings, *Kaṇaiyāḻi*,[11] the king, during darbar, *Kolu*,[12] was seated on a throne ; this was called *Kaṭṭil*,[13] and, as this name implies, was a construction of boards tied together to form a seat. Pillows, *ariaṇai*,[14] supported his back. Surrounded by his personal servants, *aḍiyār*,[15] *ūḻiyar*,[16] by heralds who proclaimed his greatness, *agavar*,[17] and by *vaḷḷuvar*,[18] publishers of royal orders, and *pāṇar*,[19] poets who sang the praises of the king, with nobles, *vaḷḷal*,[20] *aṇṇal*,[21] seated in front of him, and the common people, *āṭkaḷ*,[22] standing respectfully at a distance, the king heard complaints, dispensed justice and conducted state affairs of all kinds. The king often went out on processions, seated in a chariot, *tēr*.[23] Other names for it were *ari*,[24] *kavari*,[25] *kuyavu*,[26] *kūviram*,[27] *tigiri*,[28] *vaiyam*.[29] The royal charriot was certainly well-decorated with wood carving, for this art was practised from lithic times : the conical top of a chariot, carved to look like a lotus was called *kūmbu*,[30] *kūviram*,[31] *koḍiñji*.[32] The middle of a chariot was called *taṭṭu*,[33] or *nāppaṇ* ;[34] its floor, *pār*,[35] the boards around its body, *kiḍugu*,[36] its spoke, *ār* ;[37] the raised platform with steps near the car, from the top of which it is possible to step into the car, *muṭṭi*, [38]or *pirambu*.[39] The existence of so many names shows what an important institution the royal car was, as the temple car is now, for all the appurtenances of temple-idols are but adaptations of royal paraphernalia. The only difference between the royal car and the temple car is that the latter is drawn by human beings who desire to participate in the virtue of dragging it, but the former was drawn by bulls (*kāḷai*,[40] *erudu*,[41] *viḍai*,[42] *iṟal*[43], *ēṟu*[44], *kuṇḍai*,[45] *kūḷi*,[46] *koṭṭiyam*,[47] *kō*,[48] *chē*,[49] *pagaḍu*,[50] *pāṇḍil*,[51] *pāral*,[52] *pullam*,[53] *pūṇi*,[54] *peṟṟam*[55] *pōttu*,[56] *mūri*),[57] or by the elephant (*yānai*,[58] *kaḷiṟu*)[59]. There are

[1] பரியாரி. [2] அம்பட்டன். [3] நாவிதன். [4] மங்கலி. [5] மயிர்வினையாளன். [6] மாசுதீர்ப்போன். [7] கழல். [8] சதங்கை. [9] முத்து. [10] பவழம். [11] கணையாழி. [12] கொலு. [13] கட்டில். [14] அரியணை. [15] அடியார். [16] ஊழியர். [17] அகவர் [18] வள்ளுவர். [19] பாணர். [20] வள்ளல். [21] அண்ணல். [22] ஆட்கள். [23] தேர். [24] அரி. [25] கவரி. [26] குயவு. [27] கூவிரம். [28] திகிரி. [29] வையம். [30] கூம்பு. [31] கூவிரம். [32] கொடிஞ்சி. [33] தட்டு. [34] நாப்பண். [35] பார். [36] இடுகு. [37] ஆர். [38] முட்டி. [39] பிரம்பு. [40] காளை. [41] எருது. [42] விடை. [43] இரல். [44] ஏறு. [45] குண்டை. [46] கூளி. [47] கொட்டியம். [48] கோ. [49] சே. [50] பகடு. [51] பாண்டில். [52] பாரல் [53] புல்லம். [54] பூணி. [55] பெற்றம். [56] போத்து. [7] மூரி. [58] யானை. [59] களிறு.

about twenty[1] other names for this favourite animal, belonging to Tamil alone, besides several others for the male animal and several more for the female. The cars were decorated with flags and trappings, (*tērchchīlai*).[2]

The royal revenue, besides the proceeds from the royal lands, were derived from taxes (*vari*),[3] tolls, (*suṅgam*,[4] *uḷgu*,[5] *iṟai*),[6] and tributes (*kappam*,[7] *pariśu*,[8] *tiṟai*).[9]

Love

The chief royal occupations or amusements (for in the case of kings, it is difficult to distinguish amusements from occupations) were love and war, both of which formed the subject of innumerable odes sung by the early bards. Love and war were respectively called *agam*[10] and *puṟam*,[11] the inner life which one cannot share with other men and the outer life of action which other men can appreciate and admire. The love of kings and other men was of two kinds. (1) Love at first sight, so impetuous as to lead to immediate consummation, called *kaḷavu*,[12] to be leisurely legitimatized by a formal marriage, (*maṇam*,[13] *manṟal*,[14] *varaivu*,[15] *vēṭṭal*)[16]. (2) Post-nuptial love, called *kaṟpu*.[17] The course of love, pre-nuptial or post-nuptial, furnished the bards with innumerable incidents fit for poetic treatment and this is the subject of three chapters of the grammar of poetry, called *Poruḷadigāram*,[18] of *Tolkāppiyam*, viz., *Agattiṇaiyiyal*,[19] (referring to both),[20] *Kaḷaviyal*,[21] *Kaṟpiyal*.[22] The chief incidents of the course of both forms of love, viz., the first catastrophic meeting of the lovers called *iyaṟkaippuṇarchchi*,[23] their waiting in expectation of meeting each other, *iruttal*,[24] lamentations for temporary separation *iraṅgal*,[25] brief and long quarrels and reconciliations, *pulavi*,[26] *ūḍal*[27] and *kūḍal*,[28] and the parting of lovers, *piridal*,[29] were respectively correlated to the five natural regions, *Kuṟiñji*, *Mullai*, *Neydal*, *Marudam* and *Pālai*. The fact that Tamil literary conventions arose absolutely independent of the literary conventions of the Vedic and other early Sanskrit literature, shows that the correlations of the incidents of love with natural regions, peculiar to Tamil poetry, were based on actual customs which prevailed among the Tamil people in the third millennium B.C., and earlier. We can understand how these customs, i.e., social conventions, on which the literary conventions were based, first arose. The romantic scenery of Kuriñji land is the greatest stimulus of love and the opportunities it affords for immediate consummation fans the flame of impetuosity which is the special characteristic of Kuṟiñji love. Pre-nuptial love must have been the norm in the mountainous region, and the life of the hunter. In the Mullai region, the herdsman-lover had to be separated all day long from the mistress of his heart and hence the waiting of lovers for each other was associated with this region. In the Neydal, the woman has to sit desolate for days together, when her lover has gone on a voyage attended with risks to

[1]Such as அறுகு, ஆம்பல், இம்மடி, உம்பல், உவா, எறும்பு, ஒருத்தல், ஓங்கல், கடிவை, கள்வன், கறையடி, கைப்புலி, கைம்மலை, கைம்மா, கோட்டுமா, சுண்டாலி, குகை, திண்டி, தும்பி, தூங்கல், தெள்ளி, தோல், நால்வாய், நூழில், பகடு, புகர்முகம், புழைக்கை, பூட்கை, பெருமா, பொங்கடி, மருண்மா, மறமலி, மொய், வயமா, வல்விலங்கு, வழுவை, வேழம். [2]தேர்ச்சீலை. [3]வரி. [4]சுங்கம். [5]உலகு. [6]இறை. [7]கப்பம். [8]பரிசு. [9]திறை. [10]அகம். [11]புறம். [12]களவு. [13]மணம். [14]மன்றல். [15]வரைவு. [16]வேட்டல். [17]கற்பு. [18]பொருளதிகாரம். [19]அகத்திணையியல். [20]புறத்திணையியல். [21]களவியல். [22]கற்பியல். [23]இயற்கைப்புணர்ச்சி. [24]இருத்தல். [25]இரங்கல். [26]புலவி. [27]ஊடல். [28]கூடல். [29]பிரிதல்.

far off lands, and hence Neydal symbolizes the lamentations of lovers. So Pālai, the desert region, where the lovers have necessarily to part company, aptly symbolizes the separation of lovers. In Marudam, people led a settled agricultural and industrial life and they could enjoy longer periods of lazy leisure than the people of other regions. Hence the formal Tamil marriage-rite was evolved in Marudam.

Marriage

The ancient wedding-rite is described in the following two odes from *Agam*. 'There was a huge heap of rice cooked with pulse (even after many guests were fed). On the floor of a pandal built on long rows of wooden columns was spread freshly brought sand. House-lamps were lighted. Flower-garlands were hanging. It was the morning of the day of the bright bent (crescent) moon, when the stars shed no evil influence. Then women bearing pots on the head, others carrying new broad begging bowls handed them over one after another, fair elderly dames making much noise the while. Then four women, mothers of sons, with their pudenda marked with natural beauty-spots, wearing beautiful ornaments, poured water on the bride, so that her black hair shone bright with cool petals of flowers and rice-grains (which had been mixed with the water) and at the same time blessed her, saying, 'Do not swerve from the path of chastity, be serviceable in various ways to your husband who loves you'. On the night of the day after that of the celebration of the marriage, the neighbouring ladies assembled and said to the bride, 'Become the mistress of a great house', and she went in trepidation to the bed-room dressed in new clothes.'[1]

'Having boiled the rice free from all impurities and mixed *ghi* with it, they served it to the elders. The auspicious birds flew in the bright, beautiful, broad sky. The asterism Rohiṇi was in conjunction with the moon. They decorated the house which was free from dirt, and worshipped God. The big drum sounded, the marriage-volley was beaten. The women who desired to witness the marriage assembled in haste. The flower-eyed goddesses witnessed the marriage and disappeared. They strung on white thread the double leaf of the *agatti* which has soft flowers, many blades of the *aṛugai*-grass which

[1] உழுந்துதலைப் பெய்த கொழுங்களி மிதவை
பெருஞ்சோற் றமலை நிற்ப நிரைகாற்
றண்பெரும் பந்தர்த் தருமணன் ஞெமிரி
மனைவிளக் குறுத்து மாலை தொடரிக்
கனையிரு ளகன்ற கவின்பெறு காலைக்
கோள்கா னீங்கிய கொடுவெண் டிங்கட்
கேடில் விழுப்புகழ் நாடலை வந்தென
வுச்சிக் குடத்தர் புத்தகன் மண்டையர்
பொதுசெய் கம்பலை முதுசெம் பெண்டிர்
முன்னவும் பின்னவு முறைமுறை தரத்தரப்
புதல்வற் பயந்த திதலையவ் வயிற்று
வாலிழை மகளிர் நால்வர் கூடிக்
கற்பினின் வழாஅ நற்பல வுதவிப்
பெற்றோற் பெட்கும் பிணையை யாகென
நீரொடு சொரிந்த வீரித ழலரி
பல்லிருங் கதுப்பி னெல்லொடு தயங்க
வதுவை நன்மணங் கழிந்த பின்றைக்
கல்லென் சும்மையர் ஞெரேரெனப் புகுதந்து
பேரிற் கிழத்தி யாகெனத் தமர்தர
வோரிற் கூடிய வுடன்புணர் கங்குற்
கொடும்புறம் வளைஇக் கோடிக் கலிங்கத்
தொடுங்கினள். *Agam* 86.

the calf eats, and the young flowers of the blue water-lily which are like clean gems when the sounding rain-drops fall from the sky and adorned the bride with these garlands. Underneath a pandal strewn with sand which was cool as if rain had fallen on it, the relatives of the bride gave her away.'[1] In the ancient marriage-rite there was no circumambulation of fire, *tīvalam šeydal*,[2] which Brāhmaṇa purohitas of later ages invented in imitation of the wedding-rite of the higher varnas and introduced into the marriage-ritual of the Tamils.

In the agricultural region, there also arose *kūttiyar*[3] and *viṛaliyar*,[4] dancing-women and singing women, who were ladies of easy virtue and lived the life of *hetairae*, the *parattaiyar*,[5] who brought to a premature end the course of wedded love. Hence *ūḍal* and *kūḍal*, estrangement and reunion between husband and wife, was correlated to Marudam.

Besides these five incidents of normal love, there also existed, among the ancient Tamils, two forms of abnormal love, viz., *Kaikkiḷai*,[6] love of a man for an immature girl incapable of feeling the gentle passion, and *Perundiṇai*,[7] love of a man for a woman who does not reciprocate his love; in such a case, the man maddened with passion, made a horse of the sharp-edged stem of the palmyra, provided it with wheels and rode through the streets, bleeding, till the lady relented, or committed suicide if she did not, a proceeding technically called *Maḍalēṛudal*[8]; these are also described in many odes.

They make, of the stem of a palmyra leaf, a horse which does not require fodder, and attach to it reins adorned with small bells; the hero, wearing a garland of the short flowers of the *erukku*,[9] *calotropis gigantea*, mounts it. We drag the horse along the streets and boys gather behind and follow the procession.'[10]

'Wearing a garland in which the fresh flowers of the *āvirai*,[11] *cassia auriculata*, which resemble gold in colour, are strung on many threads,

[1] மைப்புறப் புழுக்கி னெய்க்கனி வெண்சோறு
வரையா வண்மையொடு புரையோர்ப் பேணிப்
புள்ளுப் புணர்ந்தினிய வாகத் தெள்ளொளி
யங்க ணிருவிசும்பு விளங்கத் திங்கட்
சகடம் வேண்டிய துகடீர் கூட்டத்துக்
கடிநகர் புனைந்து கடவுட பேணிப்
படுமண முழவொடு பருஉப்பணை யிமிழ
வதுவை மண்ணிய மகளிர் விதுப்புற்றுப்
பூக்கணு மிமையார் நோக்குபு மறைய
மென்பூ வாகைப் புன்புறக் கவட்டிலை
பழங்கன்று கறிக்கும் பயம்பம லறுகைத்
தழங்குரல் வானின் றலைப்பெயற் கீன்ற
மண்ணுமணி யன்ன மாயிதழ்ப் பாவைத்
தண்ணறு முகையொடு வெண்ணூல் சூட்டித்
தூவுடைப் பொலிந்து மேவரத் துவன்றி
மழைபட் டன்ன மணல்மலி பந்த
ரிழையணி சிறப்பிற் பெயர்வியர்ப் பாற்றித்
தமர்நமக் கீந்த தலைநாள். *Agam 136.*

[2] மாமுது பார்ப்பான் மறைவழி காட்டிடத்
தீவலஞ் செய்வது. *Śilappaadigāram* i.

[3] கூத்தியர். [4] விறலியர். [5] பரத்தையர். [6] கைக்கிளை. [7] பெருந்திணை. [8] மடலேறுதல். [9] எ

[10] சிறுமணி தொடர்ந்து பெருங்கச்சு நிறீஇக்
குறுமுகி ழெருக்கங் கண்ணி சூடி
புன்னூ னன்மாப் பண்ணி யெம்முடன்
மறுகுடன் றிரிதருஞ் சிறுகுறு மாக்கள்
Naṛṛinai 220.

[11] ஆவிரை.

he rides the horse made of (the stem of the leaf of) the palmyra, shame torturing his mind.'[1]

'Should I one day wearing a garland of gems on my breast and decorated with bones, go along the streets, without shame and ridiculed by others ?'[2]

These seven *tiṇais* constitute the *Agattiṇai*, the class of poems celebrating love.

WAR

The other subject of ancient poetry was war. The wars of ancient Tamil kings were not inspired by earth-hunger, for we find, throughout the ages, the boundaries of the Śera, Śōḷa, and Pāṇḍya kingdoms were intact. Wars were undertaken either as affording exercise for the development of martial virtues or for the purpose of achieving, by personal prowess, supremacy in rank and the title of the liege lord of the Tamil country and for the privilege of wearing the triple crown, *Mummuḍi*.[3] Wars were undertaken in the season which followed the harvest, when the king and the subjects had no more agricultural work to do before the next rainfall. Warlike operations were divided into five, namely, *veṭchi*,[4] *vañji*,[5] *uḻiñai*,[6] *tumbai*,[7] *vāgai*,[8] respectively corresponding to *kuṛinji*, *mullai*, *marudam*, *neydal* and *pālai*. It will be noticed that all these ten are the names of flowers and each flower symbolizes the incident which is named after it. Each of these incidents, called *tiṇai*,[9] subdivided into *tuṛai*,[10] were celebrated by people wearing garlands of flowers appropriate to it. Thus we find that the Tamils noted and named hundreds of flowers and dedicated each of them with their leaves and twigs to some separate life-situation, which they celebrated by decorating their persons with garlands of those leaves and flowers, by singing measures and dancing dances specially appropriate to each of them. The passion the Tamils had for wearing garlands, symbolic or otherwise, is further indicated by the fact that there are several words meaning garland, *kaṇṇi*,[11] *tār*,[12] *toḍaiyal*,[13] *alaṅgal*,[14] *kōdai*,[15] *teriyal*.[16] This ancient love of flowers is

[1] பொன்னே ராவிரைப் புதுமலர் மிடைந்த
பன்னூன் மாலைப் பனைபடு கலிமாப்
பூண்மணி கறங்க வேறி நாணடப்
பழிபட ருண்ணோய் வழிவழி சிறப்ப
Kuṛundogai 173.

[2] விழுத்தலைப் பெண்ணை விளையன் மாமடல்
மணியணி பெருந்தார் மார்பிற் பூட்டி
வெள்ளென் பணிந்துபிற ரெள்ளத் தோன்றி
யொருநாண் மருங்கிற் பெருநாணீக்கித்
தெருவினியலவுந் தருவது கொல்லோ?
Ib. 182.

ட. [4] வெட்சி. [5] வஞ்சி. [6] உழிஞை. [7] தும்பை. [8] வாகை. [9] திணை. [10] துறை. [11] கண்ணி. [12] தார். [13] தொடையல். [14] அலங்கல். [15] கோதை. [16] தெரியல்.

There are sixteen other names for garlands, which shows what great love the Tamils have for personal decoration with flowers. This is further indicated by the fact that garlands had differentiated names ; thus, a garland for the face was *ilambagam*,[1] *śūṭṭu*,[2] for the hair-knot, *karōḍigai*[3] ; a garland where the flowers were tied together, *śigaḻigai*,[4] *toḍaiyal*,[5] *mālai*,[6] *vāśigai*,[7] a plaited garland, *piṇaiyal* ;[8] a strung garland, *kōvai*,[9] *paḍalai*,[10] *vāśigai*.[11]

[1] இலம்பகம். [2] சூட்டு. [3] கரோடிகை. [4] சிகழிகை. [5] தொடையல். [6] மாலை. [7] வாசிகை. [8] பிணையல். [9] கோவை. [10] படலை. [11] வாசிகை.

being slowly choked out, especially in towns, by the pressure of the drab civilization of Europe, which is robbing us of many simple joys coming down from ancient times, when the love of flowers was so strong as to lead the Tamils to adopt flowers and leaves even as the distinctive uniforms of soldiers. In the battle-fields, the soldiers of each of the three great Tamil dynasties of kings could be distinguished from each other only by the garlands they wore. Thus the Pāṇḍya soldiers were decorated with the leaves and flowers of the *Vēmbu*,[1] Margosa, the Śoḷa soldiers, with those of the *Ātti*[2] or *Ār*[3], *Bauhinea racemosa*, and the Śera soldiers, of the *Panai*,[4] the palmyra. The early literature, and especially the *Tolkāppiyam*, contains frequent references to the symbolic use of leaves and flowers, and these prove that the ancient Tamils led a happy life of constant merry-making unoppressed by a too pessimistic view of the world and of man's destiny and that they were inspired by a love of nature superior in strength to that of other peoples, ancient or modern.

Of the five subdivisions of *Puṛam*, *Veṭchi*, the first, refers to the preliminary lifting of the enemy's cattle, and confining them in a pen in one's own country, which was the ancient method of the declaration of war. This proves that kingship, like formal war, began in the pastoral stage of life. As large herds of cattle are kept in the hilly region, *Veṭchi*, corresponds to *Kuṛiñji*. *Vañji* corresponds to *Mullai*; it deals with the expedition into the enemy's country, which has necessarily to pass through the wooded country surrounding the lower river valleys, where forts were built for storing in safety the accumulated agricultural and metallic wealth.

Uḻiñai has for its subject the siege of the forts, and especially the capital, of the enemy king, situated in the heart of the *Marudam* region. *Tumbai* refers to the fierce fighting which succeeds the mastery of the fort-walls, and *Vāgai*, the final victory. As *Agattinai* has on the whole seven subdivisions, so two more have been added to *Puṛattiṇai*, viz., *Kāñji*,[5] which generally deals with the transitoriness of earthly pleasures in general and the vanity of military glory in particular, the first touch of asceticism which was destined to overwhelm Indian life from the middle of the first millenium before Christ, and *Pāḍāṇ*,[6] the last of the *Puṛattiṇai*, which contains poems praising the munificence of kings and nobles towards the poets who sought their patronage.

As it was love of display of prowess and of glory that drove the ancient Tamils to war, there is no doubt that fighting was an annual institution, undertaken in the season between the gathering of the harvest and the starting of the tillage for the next year. War was called *pōr*,[7] *śaṇḍai*,[8] *śeru*,[9] *muraṇ*,[10] *tevvu*,[11] and by about twenty other words.[12] This wealth of words meaning war indicates that it was a favourite amusement with the ancient Tamils, amusement because the object of ancient war, like that of wrestling, *maṛpōr*,[13] which was thus a variety of *pōr*, was not for satisfying the lust for bloodshed, but for proving strength and skill. The field of battle was called *kaḷam*,[14]

[1] வேம்பு. [2] ஆத்தி. [3] ஆர் [4] பனை. [5] காஞ்சி. [6] பாடாண். [7] போர். [8] சண்டை [9] செரு. [10] முரண். [11] தெவ்வு. [12] அமர், ஆர்ப்பு, இகல், உறழ்வு, கணையம், கதனம், கலி, குரம்பு, கூட்டம், சமர், ஞாட்பு, தாக்கு, திறல், தும்மை, நிகம், நிகர்ப்பு, பண்டனம், மலைப்பு, மலைவு. றல், முயல், மொய், விறப்பு, வினை. [13] மற்போர். [14] களம்.

kaḷari,[1] *paṛandalai,*[2] *mudunilam* ;[3] these words also indicate waste uncultivated land, on which contests of all kinds took place and show that war did not imply the ruination of crop-bearing land. The army, *paḍai,*[4] *tānai,*[5] was divided into various groups, *aṇi,*[6] *uṇḍai,*[7] *oṭṭu* ;[8] the front ranks were *ākkam,*[9] *koḍippaḍai,*[10] *tār,*[11] *tūśi,*[12] *nirai,*[13] and the back ranks, *kūḻai.*[14] This shows that military science was not unknown to the Tamils.[15] In later times the army was divided into four sections, chariot-warriors, elephant-warriors, horse-warriors, and foot-soldiers. Of these all but the horse-arm came down from ancient times. South India was not the home of the horse and has always imported horses from the valley of the Sindhu, from Persia and other countries. But there is no doubt that the elephant was used from early times both for royal ostentation and military purposes. 'The warrior sits on an elephant, which looked like the god of death (*maṛali*). He has a broad and high breast, covered with a coat made of the tiger's skin, which the volley of arrows cannot pierce. The elephant resembles the ship that passes on the sea, the moon which moves among the stars ; it is surrounded by armed *maṛavar* like sharks, and is so excited as not to recognize its mahout.'[16] The elephants were skilfully trained and carefully looked after by the *pāgan,*[17] tied to posts, *kandu,*[18] *taṛi,*[19] in the *ālai,*[20] elephant-house, and fed with palmyrah trunks, rice and jaggery ; they were bathed in tanks or rivers, their face painted with vermilion and decorated and armoured with face-plates, *ōḍai,*[21] *suḻi.*[22] Chariots heavily decorated with wood-carving, in the profusion of which Indians revelled, and brilliantly coloured, *śāyam tōytta,*[23] trappings in various patterns and elephant warriors and foot-soldiers decked with garlands of the leaves and flowers which were the badge of each royal house, formed the serried ranks assembled on the battle-field. Of the implements of war, some came down unaltered from the Stone Age, such as the club, *taḍi,*[24] *eṛuḻ,*[25] *taṇḍu,*[26] the shorter one being *kuṇil,*[27] the bow, *vil,*[28] *kokkarai,*[29] *śilai,*[30] *taḍi,*[31] *tavar,*[32] *muni,*[33] besides the compound noun *koḍumaram*, bent-wood. Other implements were made of stone at first, and iron was substituted for stone in the early Iron Age : such as the sword, *vāḷ,*[34] *uvaṇi,*[35] *ēdi,*[36] *kaḍuttalai,*[37] *tuvaṭṭi,*[38] *navir,*[39] *nāttam,*[40] *vañjam,*[41] *vaḷ,*[42] short swords being called *kuṛumbiḍi,*[43] *śurigai,*[44] *katti,*[45] and bent ones

[2] பறந்தலை. [3] முதுநிலம். [4] படை
[8] ஒட்டு. [9] ஆக்கம். [10] கொடிப்படை. [11] தார். [12] தூசி. [13] நிரை

[15] Murugan, the Tamil war-god, who was assimilated by the northerners with the non-Vedic god Subrahmaṇya, also called Shaṇmukha, Kārttikeya, is said to have invented different forms of military formations and written a treatise on the subject in Sanskrit.

[16] புலிநிறக் கவசம் பூம்பொறி சிதைய
வெய்கணை கிழித்த பகட்டெழின் மார்பின்
மறலி யன்ன களிற்று மிசையோனே
களிறே முன்னீர் வழங்கு நாவாய் போலவும்
பன்மீ னாப்பட் டிங்கள் போலவுஞ்
சுறவினத் தன்ன வாளோர் மொய்ப்ப
மரீஇயோ ரறியாது மைந்துபட் டன்றே.

Puṛan 13

[17] பாகன். [19] தறி. [23] சாயம் தோய்த்த.
[24] தடி. [25] எறுழ். [26] தண்டு. [27] குணில். [28] வில். [30] சிலை. [31] தடி.
[32] தவர். [33] முனி. [37] கடுத்தலை. [38] துவட்டி.
[39] நவிர். [45] கத்தி.

kōṇam,[1] the spear, *īṭṭi,*[2] *iṭṭi,*[3] *kaḻukkadai,*[4] *kaḻumuḷ,*[5] the lance and the javelin, *vēl,*[6] the implement of Murugan, *eyil,*[7] *araṇam,*[8] *ehkam,*[9] [from *ehku,*[10] (1) sharp, (2) steel], *kundam,*[11] *ñāṅgar,*[12] the shorter ones being *uḍambiḍi,*[13] *viṭṭeṟu,*[14] etc.; the trident, *kaḻu,*[15] *kāḻ,*[16] the battle-axe *maḻu,*[17] *kaṇichchi,*[18] *kundāli,*[19] *kuḷir,*[20] *taṇṇam*;[21] the arrow, *ambu,*[22] *kaṇai,*[23] *kadiram,*[24] (allied to *kadir,*[25] ray, spike), *kō,*[26] *kōl,*[27] *toḍai,*[28] *tōṇi,*[29] *pagaḻi,*[30] *paḷḷam,*[31] *puḍai,*[32] *vaṇḍu,*[33] *vāḷi*;[34] the arrow being one of the earliest implements used by the Tamils in fighting with animals and men, has so many names; so too the string of the bow. *nāṇ,*[35] *nāṇi,*[36] *pūram,*[37] *āvam,*[38] *toḍai,*[39] *nāri,*[40] *narambu,*[41] *pūṭṭu,*[42] the particular point where the arrow was placed being called *uḍu.*[43] The defensive weapons were the shield, *kēḍagam,*[44] *kiḍugu,*[45] *kaḍagam,*[46] *taṭṭu,*[47] *parisai,*[48] *palagai,*[49] *maṟai,*[50] *vaṭṭaṇam,*[51] *vaṭṭam*;[52] those made of hide were distinguished as *tōl,*[53] *tōṟparam,*[54] and of cane as *taṇḍai,*[55] *vaḷḷi.*[56] A coat of armour was *mēḻagam,*[57] *araṇi,*[58] *āśu,*[59] *kandaḷam,*[60] gauntlets for protecting the hands, being called *kaippuḍai.*[61]

Musical Instruments

Drums and other musical instruments were used in warfare to inspire men and elephants (and later, horses) with martial enthusiasm. Musical instruments generally were called *iyam,*[62] *vāttiyam,*[63] *vāchchiyam,*[64] *isaikkaruvi,*[65] *iśai,*[66] being the general term for music. Musical instruments were divided into four kinds, *tōṟkaruvi,*[67] those covered with leather, *tuḷaikkaruvi,*[68] those provided with holes, *narambukkaruvi,*[69] stringed instruments, and *miḍaṟṟukkaruvi,*[70] throat-instruments. Seven names of notes belonging to Tamil are *kural,*[71] *tuttam,*[72] *kaikkiḷai,*[73] *uḻai,*[74] *iḷi,*[75] *viḷari,*[76] and *tāram,*[77] said to be produced respectively in the throat, the tongue, the palate, the head, the forehead, the pharynx, and the nose. Perhaps these are the seven notes of the scale. The chief wind-instrument was the *kuḻal,*[78] the flute, of which there were many kinds, *paṇai,*[79] made of the bamboo, *āmbal,*[80] of reed, *konṟai,*[81] of the fruit of the Cassia perforated and *mullai*, of the creeper *Jasminum trichotomum* twisted to serve as a flute. There were also different forms of the trumpet, *tārai,*[82] *kāḷam,*[83] *kākaḷam,*[84] *ammiyam,*[85] *śinnam,*[86] the cornet or horn, *kombu,*[87] *kōḍu,*[88] *iralai,*[89] *vayir.*[90]

The chief stringed instrument was the *yāḻ.*[91] There were many varieties of it, one for each of the five regions. The number of strings in the *yāḻ* varied from four to seven, sixteen, seventeen, twenty-one.

A *yāḻ* was composed of various parts: 'its *pattal*[92] (probably sounding-board) had its edges depressed and its middle raised, like the

[1]கோணம். [2]ஈட்டி. [3]இட்டி. [4]கழுக்கடை. [5]கழுமுள். [6]வேல். [7]எயில். [8]அரணம். [9]எஃகம். [10]எஃகு. [11]குந்தம். [12]ஞாங்கர். [13]உடம்பிடி. [14]விட்டேறு. [15]கழு. [16]காழ். [17]மழு. [18]கணிச்சி. [19]குந்தாலி. [20]குளிர். [21]தண்ணம். [22]அம்பு [23]கணை. [24]கதிரம். [25]கதிர். [26]கோ. [27]கோல். [28]தொடை. [29]தோணி. [30]பகழி. [31]பள்ளம். [32]புடை [33]வண்டு. [34]வாளி. [35]நாண். [36]நாணி. [37]பூரம் [38]ஆவம். [39]தொடை. [40]நாரி. [41]நரம்பு. [42]பூட்டு. [43]உடு. [44]கேடகம். [45][illegible] [46][illegible]கம். [47]தட்டு. [48]பரிசை. [49]பலகை [50]மறை. [51]வட்டணம். [52]வட்டம். [53]தோல். [54]தோற்பரம். [55]தண்டை. [56]வள்ளி. [57]மெழுகம். [58]அரணி. [59]ஆசு. [60]கந்தளம். [61]கைப்புடை. [62]இயம். [63]வாத்தியம். [64]வாச்சியம். [65]இசைக்கருவி. [66]இசை. [67]தோற்கருவி. [68]துளைக்கருவி. [69]நரம்புக்கருவி. [70]மிடற்றுக்கருவி. [71]குரல். [72]துத்தம். [73]கைக்கிளை. [74]உழை. [75]இளி. [76]விளரி. [77]தாரம். [78]குழல். [79]பணை. [80]ஆம்பல். [81]கொன்றை. [82]தாரை. [83]காளம். [84]காகளம். [85]அம்மியம். [86]சின்னம். [87]கொம்பு. [88]கோடு. [89]இரலை. [90]வயிர் [91]யாழ். [92]பத்தல்.

impression on the earth of an antelope's foot; this was covered by a skin of the colour of a flame and it was stitched in the middle and the stitches resembled the row of thin hair on the belly of a fair girl in the early stages of pregnancy; the skin was fixed to the wood by means of nails which looked like the eyes of the crab which lives in a mountain-cave; its mouth without a palate was of the shape of the moon on the eighth day after the new moon; its beam was like a serpent with its head upraised; its straps were like bracelets on the forearm of a black woman; its strings were taut and, struck by fingers looking like husked *tinai*, resounded.'[1]

In another poem it is described as having a *tol*,[2] hide of the colour of the core of the *pādiri*,[3] the trumpet flower, *Bignonia. Chelonoides*, a *tuḷai*,[4] a hole with two eyes like the bud of the *kamugu*,[5] areca-palm, a green *pōrvai*,[6] looking homogeneous as if made of melted metal, a *vāy*,[7] mouth dark like a dried up spring, a *kaḍai*,[8] extremity of the shape of the crescent, a *tivavu*,[9] bands with strips of leather, moving like the bangles at the wrists of a lady, a *maruppu*,[10] or *taṇḍu*,[11] trunk, dark like sapphire, and *narambu*,[12] strings, as if of gold.[13]

The drum, *paṛai*,[14] *muraśu*,[15] *pērigai*,[16] *āguḷi*,[17] *ellari*,[18] *śalligai*,[19] *śallari*,[20] *kiṇai*,[21] was also of various kinds and differed from region to region and also according to the purposes for which it was used. *Taḍāri*[22] or *uḍukkai*,[23] was a small double drum shaped like a sand-glass and carried by minstrels, *pāṇar*.[24] The *taṭṭai*,[25] or *karaḍigai*[26] uttered a sound like the grunt of a bear. 'Pure Tamil' names of various tunes, *paṇ*,[27] viz., *pālai*,[28] *kuṛiñji*,[29] *marudam*,[30] *śevvaḷi*,[31] occur; moreover the names of a few rāgams now sung are old Tamil names, but nothing definite about old Tamil music can be ascertained unless ancient books like the *Iśainuṇukkam*,[32] of the *Iḍaichchaṅgam*,[33] the *Śirriśai*,[34] and the *Pēriśai*,[35] of the *Kaḍaichchaṅgam*[36] are discovered.

The arms, offensive and defensive, and the drums, referred to above, were also used in hunting, *vēṭṭai*,[37] *āgēḍagam*,[38] *pābatti*.[39] which was another favourite occupation of kings and nobles. The professional shikari had numerous names, *āviyar*,[40] *kānavar*,[41] *kuṛavar*,[42]

குளப்புவழி யன்ன கவடுபடு பத்தல்
விளக்கழ லுருவின் விசியுறு பச்சை
யெய்யா விளஞ்சூற் செய்யோ ளவ்வயிற்
றைதுமயி ரொழுகிய தோற்றம் போலப்
பொல்லம் பொத்திய பொதியுறு போர்வை
யளைவாழலவன் கண்கண் டன்ன
துளைவாய் தூர்ந்த துரப்பமை யாணி
யெண்ணாட் டிங்கள் வடிவிற் றாகி
யண்ணா வில்லா வமைவரு வறுவாய்ப்
பாம்பணைத் தன்ன வோங்கிரு மருப்பின்
மாயோள் முன்கை யாய்தொடி கடுக்குங்
கண்கூ டிருக்கைத் திண்வணித் திவவி
னாய்தினை யரிசி யவைய லன்ன
வேய்வை போகிய விரலுளர் நரம்பிற்
கேள்வி போகிய நீள்விசித் தொடையல்.

Porunarāṛṛuppaḍai, 4-18.

[2]தோல். [3]பாதிரி. [4]துளை. [5]கமுகு. [6]போர்வை. வாய். [8]கடை. [9]திவவு. [10]மருப்பு. [11]தண்டு. [12]நரம்பு. [13]*Perumbāṇaṛṛuppaḍai*, 4-16. [14]பறை. [15]முரசு. [16]பேரிகை. [17]ஆகுளி. [18]எல்லரி. [19]சல்லிகை. [20]சல்லரி. [21]கிணை. [22]தடாரி. [2] உடுக்கை. [24]பாணர் [26]கரடிகை. [27]பண் [28]பாலை [29] [30]மருதம். [31]செவ்வழி. [33]இடைச்சங்கம். [34]சிற்றி [35]பேரிசை. [36]கடைச்சங்கம். [37]வேட்டை ஆகேடகம். [39]பாபத்தி. [40]ஆவியர். [41]கானவர். [42]குறவ

kunṛavar,[1] *kūḷiyar*,[2] *kolaiñar*,[3] *śavarar*,[4] *śilavar*,[5] *śillar*,[6] *tīyar*,[7] *pullar*,[8] *pulaiñar*,[9] *maṛavar*,[10] *marudar*,[11] *vēḍar*,[12] showing how widespread that profession was. They were also employed as policemen, armed with the bow and the sharp arrow.[13]

Towns and Villages: Houses

Round the *Kōṭṭai* where the king resided, grew the *pēṭṭai*,[14] (from *pē*,[15] vulgar, whence is derived *pēdai*,[16] common people, the poor, *pēy*,[17] the wild plant, also goblin). Naturally the followers of each trade gravitated towards each other and each principal profession was confined to a single pēṭṭai; there were thus many suburbs around a town, separated from each other. These pēṭṭais were each surrounded by rice-fields or gardens. There are many words to indicate a house, such as *vīḍu*,[18] *agam*,[19] *il*,[20] *illam*,[21] *śērbu*,[22] *pātti*,[23] *manai*,[24] *vayin*,[25] besides the compound words *uṛaiyuḷ*[26] and *pukkiḷ*.[27] The houses of richer men were called *māḍam*[28] (whence perhaps *māḍi*,[29] upper story) or *māḷigai*[30] from the root *māḷ*,[31] great. They were built almost entirely of timber up to about twelve centuries ago. The following words relating to parts of a house may be noted: *iṛappu*,[32] *iṛai*,[33] *vaḷavu*,[34] *tāḻvāram*,[35] sloping roof; *munṛil*,[36] *muṛṛam*,[37] courtyard, inside or outside a house; the compound word *nilāmuṛṛam*,[38] a flat roof on which one can walk up and down; *uttiram*,[39] *tūlam*,[40] beam *suṛṛuvāri*,[41] *tāḻ*,[42] *tuḍai*,[43] *mugaḍu*,[44] *viḍaṅgam*,[45] beam projecting beyond a wall. In front of the houses was the *tiṇṇai*[46] a raised and covered platform, which served the purposes of a drawing-room and bed-room for the day and even for the night. Before the *tiṇṇai*, was the *kuṛadu*,[47] open platform, flanked by the *oṭṭuttiṇṇai*.[48] The walls, the *tiṇṇai* and the floor of the house were no doubt polished like a mirror or black-marble, the cement being compounded of clay, charcoal and cattle-dung, *maṇ*,[49] *kari*,[50] and *śāṇi*,[51] and applied to the surface wet and rubbed over for hours with a bit of flattened quartz, an art which is fast dying out. The entrance to the house was not flush with street, as there was a *vāyilpaḍi*,[52] door-step. It was provided with a wooden frame work, *nilai*,[53] and a door, *kadavu*,[54] also called *araṇam*,[55] *aravam*,[56] *kāppu*,[57] *tōṭṭi*,[58] *pudavu*,[59] *vāri*,[60] secured by a wooden bolt and heavily carved outside, as they are even to-day in houses not ruined by modern civilization. The houses were provided with windows, *śāḷaram*,[61] *śannal*,[62] *palagaṇi*,[63] being, as the name implied, a many-eyed lattice window. Behind the door ran a narrow passage, *iḍaikaḻi*,[64] or *naḍai*,[65] which led into the house. The houses were provided with

[1] குன்றவர். [2] கூளியர். [3] கொலைஞர். [4] சவரர். [5] சிலவர். [6] சில்ல [7] தீயர். [8] புல்லர். [9] புலைஞர். [10] மறவர். [11]

[13] கூர்நல் அம்பின் கொடுவில் கூளியர்.

Malaipaḍukaḍām, 422.

[14] பேட்டை. [15] பே [16] பேதை. [17] பேய். [18] வீடு. [19] அகம். [20] இல். [21] இல்லம். [22] சேர்ப்பு. [23] பாத்தி. [24] மனை. [25] வயின். [26] உறையுள். [27] புக்கில். The houses of Brāhmaṇas were given the Sanskrit name of *Aharam* (ஆகரம) and the street where they lived *akkirāhāram* (அக்கிரகாரம்.)

[28] மாடம். [29] (மா)டி. [30] மாளிகை [31] மாள். [32] இறப்பு. [33] இறை. [34] வளவு. [35] தாழ்வாரம். [36] முன்றில். [37] முற்றம் [38] நிலாமுற்றம். [39] உத்திரம். [40] தூலம். [41] சுற்றுவாரி. [42] தாழ். [43] து [44] முகடு. [45] விடங்கம். [46] திண்ணை. [47] குறடு. [48] ஒட்டுத்திண்ணை. [49] மண். [51] சாணி. [52] வாயில்படி. [53] நிலை. [54] கதவு. [55] அரணம். [56] அரவம். [57] காப்பு. [58] தோட்டி. [59] புதவு. [60] வரி. [61] சாளரம். [62] சன்னல். [63] பலகணி. [64] இடைகழி. [65] நடை.

drains, *śākkaḍai,*[1] or *śālagam,*[2] as were the houses of Mohenjo-daro, recently unearthed. The spout of the drain was *tūmbu,*[3] *puḻal,*[4] *śuruṅgu.*[5] The inside walls were provided with niches, *purai,*[6] in which were placed, among other things, the lamps to light the house by night. These lamps were little bowls of stone or earthern-ware, or metal, *agal,*[7] *tagaḷi,*[8] *tagaḻi,*[9] *iḍiñjil,*[10] *pāṇḍil,*[11] in which castor oil or other oils were burnt with a cotton wick.[12] Behind the house was another *kuṟadu,*[13] which was a lumber room. Behind this the house-well, *kiṇaṟu,*[14] *aśumbu,*[15] *uṟavi,*[16] *kuḻi,*[17] *kūval,*[18] *kūḍam,*[19] *tuṟavu,*[20] *kēṇi.*[21] *pūval,*[22] the latter three being water pits without a protecting structure of wood around them. Behind the well stretched a garden, either a kitchen garden or a fruit tope, *kollai,*[23] *tōppu,*[24] *tōṭṭam,*[25] *āvalam,*[26] *tuḍavai,*[27] *toḍuvu,*[28] *paḍappai,*[29] *pāvagam,*[30] *punam.*[31] In the *kollai* behind the house was the *koṭṭil,*[32] cattle-shed, *koṭṭu,*[33] from probably the same word as Telugu *goḍḍu,* cattle, and *il,* meaning house. Behind the garden stretched the corn fields, *vayal.*[34]

The furniture of houses was utensils for polishing and grinding rice and for cooking it in various ways. *Ural*[35] and *ullakkai*[36] mortar and pestle, of both wood and stone, pounding stones of several shapes, sometimes the shape of the tortoise or other animals, *ammi,*[37] *tiruvai*[38] *āṭṭukkal,*[39] *kuḻavi,*[40] mealers of stone, *puṭṭil,*[41] *vaṭṭigai,*[42] basket, *muṟam,*[43] *śinnam,*[44] *suḷagu,*[45] *taṭṭu,*[46] *muṟṟil,*[47] winnowing fan, *sallaḍai,*[48] sieve ; different forms of pots of earthenware or soft stone, *pānai.*[49] *śaṭṭi,*[50] *śāl,*[51] *kuḍam,*[52] *miḍā,*[53] *pānā,*[54] *mallāy,*[55] lid for the same, *maḍakku* ;[56] spoons, at first made of wood, and then of iron or other metal, *agappai,*[57] (of three kinds, *taṭṭagappai,*[58] *sandagappai,*[59] *śiṟṟagappai,*[60]) *śaṭṭuvam,*[61] *karaṇḍi,*[62] *muṭṭai, tuḍuppu,*[63] *maravai,*[64] *marakkāl,*[65] or *ambaṇam,*[66] *toṭṭi,*[67] *kiṇṇam,*[68] *vaṭṭi,*[69] *vaṭṭil,*[70] flat spoon, all of wood or stone coming down from the stone age and a few of metal since the commencement of the iron age ; other household furniture were *maṇai,*[71] planks for sitting on or shaped logs used as pillows, *peṭṭi,*[72] *pēḻai,*[73] *mañjikai,*[74] box, the stone-age form of which was the *kaṭṭuppeṭṭi,*[75] a box of wicker work without any metal parts and bound together by means of cocoanut coir, and hence absolutely unpollutable by touch and fit for storing eatables and the Lares and Penates ; *kaṭṭil,*[76] literally bound place, a cot made of bamboos fitted together into an oblong framework bound together with ropes, also called *pāṇḍil* ;[77] literature mentions richer forms of

[1] சாக்கடை. [2] சாலகம். [3] தூம்பு. [4] புழல். [5] சுருங்கு. [6] புரை. [7] அகல். [8] தகளி. [9] தகழி. [10] இடிஞ்சில். [11] பாண்டில் [12] பஞ்சி வெண்டிரிச் செஞ்சுடர் நல்லில், *Kuṟundogai*, 353. A good house with red flames issuing from white wicks of cotton wool. [13] குறடு. [14] கிணறு. [15] அசும்பு. [16] உறவி. [17] குழி. [18] கூவல். [19] கூடம். [20] துறவு. [21] கேணி. [22] பூவல். [23] கொல்லை. [24] தோப்பு. [25] தோட்டம். [26] ஆவலம். [27] துடவை [28] தொடுவு. [29] படப்பை. [30] பாவகம். [31] புனம். A new *kollai* was *vidaippunam*, (விதைப்புனம்.) and an old one, or one made by cutting and burning down a forest, *mudaippunam* (முதைப்புனம்.) [32] கொட்டில். [33] கொட்டு. [34] வாயில். [35] உரல். [36] உலக்கை [37] அம்மி. [38] திருவை. [39] ஆட்டுக்கல். [40] குழவி. [41] புட்டில். [42] வட்டிகை. [43] முறம். [44] சின்னம். சுளகு. [46] தட்டு. [47] முற்றில். [48] சல்லடை. [49] பானை. [50] சட்டி. [51] சால். [52] குடம். [53] மிடா. [54] பா [55] மல்லாய். [56] மடக்கு. [57] அகப்பை. [58] தட்டகப்பை. [59] சந்தகப்பை. [60] சிற்றகப்பை [61] சட்டுவம். [62] கரண்டி. [63] துடுப்பு. [64] மரவை. [65] மரக்கால். [66] அம்பணம். [67] தொட்டி. [68] கிண்ணம். டி. [70] வட்டில். [71] மணை. [72] பெட்டி. *Tapalai, tavalai,* and *śaṟuvam* are now used for metal pots and are perhaps loan-words of a later age. [73] பேழை. [74] மஞ்சிகை. [75] கட்டுப்பெட்டி. [76] கட்டில். [77] பாண்டில்.

the *pāṇḍil*, which will be described later on, tied with tape, *taṭṭam*,[1] or *kachchu*,[2] woven with decorative lines, like the stripes of a tiger; this kind of cot was called *kachchukkaṭṭil*,[3] the former being *kayiṟṟuk-kaṭṭil*.[4]

Besides the cot there was the *toṭṭil*,[5] cradle, literally, hanging place, (from *to*,[6] whose intensive is *toṅgu*,[7] to hang,) *tūḷi*,[8] hammock, *ūñjal*[9] or *vīśupalagai*,[10] swinging plank, *kuḍalai*[11] plaited basket for gathering flowers, *śimiḻ*,[12] small casket, *uṟi*,[13] or *śimili*,[14] a loop of string suspended from the roof of a house or from the end of a pole called *kāvaḍi*,[15] by means of which one man can carry two men's loads; *kaṇappu*,[16] or *kumbaṭṭi*[17] for warming the hands and the breast during cold nights, *paṭṭaḍai*,[18] *śumuḍu*,[19] *śummāḍu*,[20] contrivances on which to stand pots *kūḍu*,[21] coop, *kuḍir*,[22] granary, *paraṅ*,[23] *idaṇam*,[24] *kaḻuḍu*,[25] *paḍagam*,[26] *paṇavai*,[27] loft for storing articles, also raised platform for watching birds and other enemies of the growing crops, *taḍavu*,[28] *indaḷam*,[29] censer, *ñelikōl*,[30] stick for churning fire, *tūkku*,[31] *kā*,[32] *niṟaikol*,[33] steelyard introduced into Europe by the Dutch and hence called Dutch steel-yard, *kavaṇ*,[34] *taḻal*,[35] sling, also bull-roarer; *pāy*,[36] mat, and *mettai*,[37] *aṇai*,[38] *amaḷi*,[39] *kāguḷi*,[40] *taviśu*,[41] *taḷimam*,[42] bed stuffed with cotton. These constitute, even now, the complete furniture of Tamil homes such as have not come under the seductive influence of European foreign trade.

The poorer people lived in huts, *kuḍiśai*,[43] *kuḍil*,[44] *kuchchu*,[45] *kuchchil*,[46] *kurambai*.[47] Their walls were made of wattle and clay, and they were generally circular, rarely rectangular, in shape; the roof was rarely aspidal, but mostly domical and topped by a pot, *kuḍam*,[48] through a hole in which were passed the bamboos constituting the framework of the roof; and from the early days when such huts were built, temples were built in similar fashion, and when later they were built of brick or stone, over the shrines was built a domical roof, furnished with a metal pot, now called *kalaśam*[49] and serving an ornamental, not useful, purpose.

The following is a description of a hunter's hut of old times:—

'In the huts of the hunters were leaning, on the planks decorated with bells, lances whose ends were blunted and smelling of flesh from the bodies of enemies whom the hunters killed and left lying on the ground, a prey for kites. Bows with the string tied in knots were also leaning on the walls on which there was a thatch of *ūga*[50] grass. Bundles of arrows with notches like honeycombs on hills were hanging from the thick legs of the pandal. The huts were guarded by dogs chained to posts. The compound was surrounded by a living hedge of thorns. The door was fastened by a strong beam. In front were

1 தட்டம். 2 கச்சு. 3 கச்சுக்கட்டில். 4 கயிற்றுக்கட்டில். 5 தொட்டில். 6 தொ. 7 தொங்கு 8 தூளி. 9 ஊஞ்சல். 10 வீசுபலகை. 11 குடலை. 12 சிமிழ். 13 உறி. 14 சிமிலி. 15 காவடி. 16 கணப்பு. 17 கும்பட்டி. 18 பட்டடை. 19 சுமுடு. 20 சும்மாடு. 21 கூடு. 22 குதிர். 23 பரண். 24 இதணம். 25 கழுது. 26 படகம். 27 பணவை. 28 தடவு. 29 இந்தளம். 30 ஞெலிகோல். 31 தூக்கு. 32 கா. 33 நிறைகோல். 34 கவண். 35 தழல். 36 பாய். 37 மெத்தை. 38 அணை 39 அமளி. 40 காகுளி. 41 தவிசு. 42 தளிமம். 43 குடிசை. 44 குடில். 45 குச்சு. 46 குச்சில். 47 குரம்பை. 8 குடம். 49 கலசம். ஊகம்.

fixed rows of stiff-standing, cruel-pointed stakes. Such were the houses of the hunters who were armed with the bent bow.'[1]

More or less irregular rows or groups of *kudiśais*,[2] huts, sparsely interspersed with *māḷigais*,[3] constituted the street, *teru*,[4] *āvaṇam*,[5] *kōśam*,[6] *ñellal*,[7] *maṟugu*;[8] a long street was called *manṟam*,[9] a short one, *kōṇam*,[10] and the place where many streets meet, *śadukkam*,[11] or *sandu*.[12] Towns and villages were named variously according to the regions, *tiṇai*,[13] they belonged to. Thus in Kuṟiñji, they were called *śiṟukudi*,[14] *kuṟichchi*;[15] in Mullai, *pāḍi*,[16] *śēri*,[17] *paḷḷi*;[18] in Marudam, *ūr*;[19] in Neydal, *pākkam*;[20] and in Pālai, *paṟan-dalai*.[21] In the towns dwelt, side by side, *mēlōr*[22] or *uyarndōr*[23] and *kīḻor*[24] or *tāḻndōr*,[25] the higher and the lower classes. The later literature of the early Christian centuries speak of two assemblies of men who were the recipients of royal confidence—*aimberukuḻu*[26] and *eṇpērāyam*.[27] *kuḻu*[28] and *āyam*[29] meant assemblies; the five assemblies have been explained by commentators as those of ministers, priests, army leaders, ambassadors and intelligence officers, but the names of these, viz., *amaichchar*,[30] *purōhitar*,[31] *sēnāpadiyar*,[32] *tūduvar*[33] and *śāraṇar*[34], are all *tadbhavas* from Sanskrit and hence it is difficult to decide that the five groups of officers existed from old times. The group of eight are said to consist of ministers, executive officers, treasury officers, door-keepers, citizens, generals, elephant-warriors, horse-soldiers.[35] This enumeration, mixing men of high and low degree, does not strike one as referring to very ancient times. An early commentator of *Śilappadigāram* gives a less improbable enumeration of these five and eight assemblies; the five are made up of sages, Brahmans, physicians, soothsayers and ministers; even this cannot be a classification of the Pre-Aryan Epoch because Brāhmaṇas occurs in the list. The eight are those who apply sandal paste to the person of the king, those that decorate him with flowers, those that

[1]பருந்துபட
வொன்னாத் தெவ்வர் நடுங்க வோச்சி
வைந்நுதி மழுங்கிய புலவுவாய் எஃகம்
வடிமணிப் பலகையொடு நிரைஇ முடியரண்
சாபஞ் சாத்திய கணைதுஞ்சு வியனகர்
ஊகம் வேய்ந்த உயர்நிலை வரைப்பின்
வரைத்தேன் புரையும் கவைக்கடைப் புதையொடு
கடுந்துடி தூங்கும் கணைக்கால் பந்தர்த்
தொடர்நாய் யாத்த துன்னருங் கடிநகர்
வாழ்முள் வேலிச் சூழ்மிளைப் படப்பைக்
கொடுநுகத் தழீஇய புதவிற் செந்நிலை
நெடுநுதி வயக்கழு நிரைத்த வாயிற்
கொடுவில் லெயினர் குறும்பு.

Perumbāṇāṟṟuppaḍai. 117—129.

[2]குடிசை. [3]மாளிகை. [4]தெரு. [5]ஆவணம். [6]கோசம். [7]ஞெல்லல். [8]மறுகு. [9]மன்றம். [10]கோணம். [11]சதுக்கம். [12]சந்து. [13]திணை. [14]சிறுகுடி. [15]குறிச்சி. [16]பாடி. [17]சேரி. [18]பள்ளி. [19]ஊர். [20]பாக்கம். [21]பறந்தலை. [22]மேலோர். [23]உயர்ந்தோர். [24]கீழோர். [25]தாழ்ந்தோர். [26]ஐம்பெருங்குழு. [27]எண்பேராயம். [28]குழு. [29]ஆயம். [30]அமைச்சர். [31]புரோகிதர். [32]சேனாபதியர். [33]தூதுவர். [34]சாரணர் அமைச்சர் புரோகிதர் சேனைபதியர் தவாத்தொழிற் றூதுவர் சாரணரென்றிவர் பார்த்திபர்க் கைம்பெருங் குழுவெனப்படுமே. *Divākaram* 163.

[35]காரணத்தியலவர் கருமவிதிகள், கனகச்சுற்றங்கடை காப்பாளர், நகரமாந்தர் நளிபடைத்தலைவர், யானைவீரர் இவுளிமறவ ரினையரெண்பே ராயமென்ப. *Ib.* quoted in the commentaries on *Śilappadigāram*, v. 157, p. 144.

fasten his belt, those that clothe him, those that supply arecanut and betel leaves and those that put on his armour.'[1] This looks like a genuine list of the persons immediately round the king.

DRESS

The cotton plant is a native of India and the Indians of the later stone age learnt to spin the cotton fibre into thread, *nūl*,[2] *iḻai*,[3] *saradu*,[4] *todar*,[5] *nuvaṇam*,[6] *panuval*,[7] *piśin*,[8] and to weave cotton yarn into long pieces of cloth. The idea of cloth was no doubt suggested by *pannāḍai*[9], also called *neyyari*[10] which the people wore, besides hides, before the invention of cotton-weaving. *Pannāḍai* is the web at the bottom of a young palmyra or cocoanut leaf and was used as cloth in very ancient times, for *maravuri*,[11] tree-flay, also called *āśini*, [12] *iṟaiñji*, [13] *śīram*, [14] *sīrai*, [15] is one of the forms of dress which possesses the holiness of hoary antiquity and is patronized by sacred ascetics and pilgrims. The supply of cotton was abundant and weavers wore endless lengths of cotton cloth, *tugil*, [16] which they cut into short pieces, *aṟuvai*, [17] *tuṇi*, [18] *tuṇḍu* [19] before winding round their persons. The number of words meaning dress is very great: *āśāram*, [20] *āsiḍai*,[21] *āḍai*,[22] *iḍaidal*, [23] *ilakkāram*, [24] *uḍukkai* [25] *uḍai*,[26] *eḍagam*, [27] *oliyal*, [28] (specially used for *mēlāḍai*, cloth worn over the shoulder), *kandai*, [29] *kattiyam*, [30] *kappaḍam*, [31] *kalai*, [32] *kāḍagam*, [33] *kāṇḍam*, [34] *kāḻagam*,[35] *kūṟai*,[36] (now used for cloth, presented to the bride during marriage), *kōḍi* [37] (now used for cloth, unwashed, straight from the hands of the weaver or the vendor), *śambaran*, [38] *sāḍi*, [39] *siṟṟil*,[40] *śirai*, [41] *śūḍi*, [42] *śēlai*, [43] *tānai* [44] (also *mēlaḍai*), *tūśu*, [45] *tūṭṭi*, [46] *tūriyam*, [47] *tokkai*, [48] *miḍiyal*,[49] *pudavai*,[50] (now restricted to the long piece of cloth worn by women), *paḍām*,[51] *paṭṭam* ;[52] and many others. All these words meant cloth woven of the fibre of cotton. Those woven of silk were called *karambu*,[53] *paṇi*.[54] *paraṇam*, [55] *pāḷidam*,[56] and woollen cloth, *mayiragam*, [57] *vayiriyam*.[58] The fewness of the names of silk and woollen cloth shows that weaving in these was scarce. Cloth dyed in various colours, *śāyam toytta*,[59] was freely used. Indeed decoration being the chief aim of Indian art, as will be explained later, plain white cloth was considered as fit for occasions of mourning and for being worn by women in permanent mourning, i.e., widows. Hence dyed cloth and that decorated with flowers on the borders and throughout the body of the cloth was the usual wear. A much decorated cloth,

[1] சாந்தும் பூவும் கச்சாடை பாக்கிலை கஞ்சுகம்
பாய்ந்த விவரெண்ம ராயத்தோர் — வேந்தர்க்கு
மாசனம் பார்ப்பார் மருத்தர் வாழ்நிமித்த ரோடமைச்ச
ராகிலவைக் களத்தாரைந்து. *op. cit.* p. 144.

[2] நூல். [3] இழை. [4] சரடு. [5] தொடர் [6] நுவணம். [7] பனுவல். [8] பிசின். [9] பன்னாடை. [10] நெய்யரி. [11] மரவுரி. [12] ஆசினி. [13] இறைஞ்சி. [14] சீரம். [15] சீரை [16] துகில். [17] அறுவை, from root அறு to cut. [18] துணி. [19] துண்டு, both from root துண் to cut. [20] ஆசாரம். [21] ஆசிடை. [22] ஆடை. [23] இடைதல். [24] இலக்காரம். [25] உடுக்கை. [26] உடை. [27] எடகம். [28] ஒலியல். [29] கந்தை. [30] கத்தியம். [51] கப்படம். [32] கலை. [33] காடகம். [34] காண்டம். [35] காழகம். [36] கூறை. கோடி. [38] சம்பரம். [39] சாடி [40] [41] சீரை. [42] சூடி. [43] சேலை. [44] தானை. [45] தூசு. [46] தூட்டி. [47] [48] தொக்கை. [49] மிடியல். [50] புட [51] படாம். [52] பட்டம். [53] [55] பரணம். பாளிதம். [57] மயிரகம், [58] வயிரியம். [59] சாயம்தோய்த்த.

woven so finely that the yarn could not be distinguished by sight an adorned with woven flowers so that it looked like the skin of the serpent is refered to in literature.[1] The sentiment against plain, white, undecorated cloth was so strong even two generations ago, when machine-made cloth began to compete vigorously with hand-woven cloth, that the more conservative of the men, who were tempted to use Manchester mull on account of its cheapness, stitched across its borders and along its edges, lines of red thread to make it look respectable. Even to-day the old instincts assert themselves on occasions of festive celebrations, when undecorated cloth is taboo. This objection to undecorated cloth, yards of unrelieved whiteness, this sentiment springing from age-long association of plain, undyed, undecorated cloth with mourning and the offensiveness of its monotony to eyes trained to a sense of beauty and to the æsthetic instincts common to all Indians, has in the last two generations been vanquished by the glamour of machine-made cloth, woven of yarn spun evenly by spinning machines and polished by chemical appliances, ever-new forms of which are being invented day after day. Tamil ladies alone have presented a solid front of opposition to this destruction of the æsthetic sense of South Indians by soul-less, machine-made cloth.

Weaving in wool is as ancient as weaving in cotton ; it was essentially an industry, not of *marudam*, but of *mullai*, in the less fertile parts of which lived the *Kuṛumbar*,[2] the class of herdsmen who tended the *kuṛumbāḍu*,[3] and wove from its fleece the *kambaḷam*,[4] ten thousands years ago as they do to-day. Wool weaving did not go beyond its crude stage in Southern India ; but in Northern India, and especially in Kashmir, where the supply of soft wool from the necks of Himalayan goats was unlimited and where vegetation on the banks of hill-streams and beds of flowers on mountain-sides, presented ever varying patterns to be incorporated by the weaver in wool, was developed the splendid industry of shawl-weaving, which will never be killed by the greatest growth of machine-weaving, so long as man has eyes to see beautiful forms and sense to appreciate beautiful designs.

Silk was used chiefly for decorating the edges of cotton cloth, since the silk fibre was not abundant ; but from the earliest times cloth was also wholly woven of silk thread ; silk cloth and woollen cloth are less susceptible of the pollution of touch than cotton cloth, showing that they were older manufactures than the latter. A cloth woven from rat's hair is also mentioned.[5] But cotton cloth was peculiarly sensitive to touch, in the sense that it could be easily polluted. Every piece of cotton cloth, doffed, *viḻutta*,[6] after wear even for a second became *viḻuppu*,[7] polluted, and the pollution could be got rid of only after being washed with water, dried in air and folded, when it became *maḍi*.[8] This last word meaning fold, came to mean a cloth,

[1] நோக்கு நுழைகல்லா நுண்மைய பூக்கனிந் தரவுரியன்ன வறுவை. *Porunarāṟṟuppaḍai*, 82.83.
[2] குறும்பர். [3] குறும்பாடு. [4] கம்பளம்.

[5] *Śilappadigāram*, xiv. 205–7 speaks of the streets where were sold, cloth folded a hundred-fold, woven of fine cotton yarn, hair and silk thread ; here the commentator explains hair to be rats' hair.
"நூலினு மயிரினு நுழைநூற் பட்டினும், பால்வகை தெரியாப் பன்னூறடுக்கத்து நறுமடி, செறிந்த வறுவை வீதியும்"

[6] விழுத்த. [7] விழுப்பு. [8] மடி.

sacramentally pure, when folded after being washed and dried. Such cloth was unfolded and worn, a long piece around the waist and another, round the trunk, loose and graceful, beautiful to look at and allowing the air and the sun to kiss the skin and destroy the innumerable germs that get lodged in it and destroy its health. The supply of cotton being unlimited and the patience of the weavers being inexhaustible, there was no temptation, such as existed in wool-wearing countries, to cut up cloth so as to make small bits go a long way, and to prepare stitched clothes. Not that the needle (*ūsi.*[1] *ilai-vāngi,*[2]) or its use in stitching, *tunnal,*[3] *taiyal,*[4] was unknown,[5] but in addition to the objection that stitched clothes reveal too much the human anatomy, there was no necessity to use them when cloth was plentiful. Indeed whole cloth, without a tear, mended or unmended, became in popular estimation sacramentally pure, and stitches of any kind rendered cloth unfit for use on ceremonial occasions. Ladies who in all respects preserve ancient orthodoxy intact, do not wear stitched cloth on such occasions. The jacket, the only form of stitched clothes ladies wear, has got the non-Tamil name of *ravikkai*;[6] it was possibly introduced into the country by Yavana (Greek and Roman) ladies that formed the body-guard of Indian kings two thousand years ago, or later by the Muhammadans. Whatever its origin, it is worn only on secular occasions and even then only by young women, who are allowed greater lapses into heterodoxy of conduct than elderly ladies. Serving men and soldiers wore coats, *śaṭṭai,*[7] *kuppāyam,*[8] *taippai,*[9] *meyppai,*[10] the latter two *kāraṇappeyar*, indicating that a coat was a late introduction in the lives of the Tamils. The absence of stitched clothes among the Indians struck that accurate foreign student of Indian manners, Al Bērūni, as so peculiar, that he remarks that the Indians 'wore turbans for trousers,' a long piece of unstitched cloth appealing to the Muslim imagination as being fit only for turbans. The Tamils did not wear turbans as a rule, their unshaved head serving as sufficient protection against the sun; but in the cotton districts where the summer sun is so fierce, men wore huge turbans and tight fore-lap cloth. This latter, *kachchu,*[11] *kachchai,*[12] *kōvaṇam,*[13] is the only absolutely indispensable garment for the Tamil people, and is woven with decorative lines, athwart and along, even to-day in parts of South India. Apparently the turban was not universal; only one name for it is traceable—*pāgai,*[14] or *pāgu,*[15] often with *talai,*[16] prefixed to it, it is not possible to guess why. There remain *kuḍai,*[17] umbrella, made of palm leaves and fixed to a stick or clapped on the head like a hat, and *śeruppu,*[18] leather sandals and *kuradu,*[19] wooden sandals, for the feet, both also being referred to by the compound word *midiyaḍi.*[20]

[1] ஊசி. [2] இலைவாங்கி. [3] துன்னல். [4] தையல்.

[5] A poor man's rags are described in *Porunarāṟṟuppaḍai*, 80–81, as cloth stitched, full of threads other than those with which it was woven and wet with sweat.

வேரொடு நனைந்த வேற்றிழை நுழைந்த, துன்னற் சிதா அர்.

[6] ரவிக்கை. [7] சட்டை. [8] குப்பாயம். [9] தைப்பை. [10] மெய்ப்பை. [11] கச்சு. [12] கச்சை. [13] கோவணம். [14] பாகை. [15] பாகு. [16] தலை. [17] குடை. [18] செருப்பு. [19] குறடு. [20] மிதியடி.

Decoration

The artistic instincts of the Indian people expressed themselves in the form of personal decoration by means of dress and ornaments. Love of decorating not only the person but of every article, has been the inspiring motive of Indian art throughout the ages. Their dwellings were decorated with colour drawings, as is proved by the fact that palettes, and pencils have been found in Stone Age settlements and that even to-day painting on walls and covering the floor daily inside and outside houses with most elaborate designs in coloured powders is practiced. The custom is so old that only on occasions of a death in the house, is it temporarily suspended. Such adornment of the floor is called *kōlam*,[1] which word means beauty, ornaments, embellishments, costumes, trappings, and *kōlam buṉaippeṉ*,[2] or *vaṇṇamagaḷ*,[3] is the girl who is expert in embellishment, also a lady's dressing maid. This is one of many ancient Indian customs that is dying out on account of the impact of Western civilization; our ladies are struggling to keep up the custom, but our young girls are being no more apprenticed to our matrons for being trained as *kōlam buṉaippeṉ*. As the soul-less 'type-design' buildings constructed by the D.P.W., are destroying taste in architecture, so the education that is given in our girls' schools is killing out the ancient Indian art of house decoration, which now exists only in the villages round celebrated temples and which can be witnessed only on occasions when the temple God is brought out in procession.

Every article of domestic furniture was decorated with art work. Stone articles were made in the shape of tortoises, fishes, heads of cows, etc. and their surface decorated with lines. All articles of wood were filled with wood-carving in various designs. Most of these designs were based on the parts of the lotus plant. The lotus is a plant, every part of which is useful to man; its flower, its seed, its root and its stem are edible and also used in Indian medicine. Its stem and flowers and leaves are used for purposes of decoration. Hence the shape of its leaf and flower and of its stem and seed were combined in various ways to make designs for carving in wood or metal. Every part of the house was ornamented with such carvings: the door-frame, the doors, beam-ends, every part of a pillar, its base, its body, its cornice, was filled with beautiful carvings. When stone was substituted for wood as material for all this work, designs for wood-carving were transferred to stone, though it is very difficult to copy on stone the kind of carving suited to wood.

Not only fixtures but also all movable articles were filled with decorative carving. Sitting and other planks had many designs cut on them; lotus flowers, cut in metal, were used to make them look pleasing to the eye. All household utensils of wood or metal were works of art. Drinking vessels and water-pots were not only made of the most artistic shapes but were decorated with line-drawing and carving; this continues to be so except in towns where the ugly machine-made products of modern European factories are slowly displacing the products of ancient Indian art-work and the artistic sense of the Indian people being slowly choked out.

[1] கோலம். [2] கோலம் புனைப்பெண். [3] வண்ணமகள்.

The humblest tool used by the ancient Indian was made of a beautiful shape and was besides decorated ; the humble bill book, *arivāl*,[1] which is hooked on to the waist-string of the labourer, is not only of a beautiful shape, but is provided with leaf shaped notches and the brass ferule which binds it to its handle is decorated with art work. The vegetable knife, used in every house, *arivāḷmaṇai*,[2] has its iron part shaped to resemble a bird and its wooden part covered with line-design. No Indian workman will finish any work of his hands, small or big, humble or otherwise, without putting on it some bit of art work. The country cart, cumbrous as it looks to the careless observer, has every part of it, including the beam, *achchu*,[3] on which the frame-work rests and which holds or does duty for the axle-tree is filled with carvings of the lotus flower or the lotus leaves or stems. The rich carvings on temple-cars which are but copies of ancient wood temples, are too well known to require description here.

The extraordinary development of wood-carving (succeeded by stone-carving) in preference to other forms of art in India was due to two causes. Hard woods that lent themselves to most minute carving grew in abundance. But the more important cause is that the aim of Indian art is decorative and not imitative. Ancient Greek art had for its aim the imitation of the forms of men and of natural objects ; the nearer the copy was to the original, the more successful was the art product claimed to be. The art work was executed for its own sake, because as Keats said, ' a thing of beauty is a joy for ever'. Hence art was an end in itself and art-objects were not considered decorations of the drawing room or of something other than themselves. Thus the famous frescoes which exist in various parts of the country are but decorations of cave temples and cave-monasteries, just as carving and group-statuary in stone, in stucco, or in wood, are but decorations of the *vimānam*,[4] *gōpuram*,[5] or the car of the temple. Hence whereas pictures or statues which belong to Greek art are individual objects, those belonging to Indian art are extensive compositions, stories in paint, or stone or wood. Greek art aims at perfection of form, because each art-product exists by itself : Indian art aims at representation of life and moving objects and not still life, because each figure is but the part of an extensive composition. Self-restraint is the chief characteristic of the Greek art, but the Indian artist lets himself go without any restriction on the outflow of his genius. As a singer when performing *ālāpanam*[6] of a *rāgam*,[7] takes a theme and rings endless changes on it, as many as his throat is capable of producing, as a poet, started on a description, seems never to be able to exhaust his subject, so the painter and the carver is never tired of multiplying details in the exposition of the central idea. Foreigners do the greatest injustice possible to Indian art when they take away from their proper place pieces of the stone work of Bharhut or Amarāvati, bits of paintings from Ajanta or Ellora, and judge them divorced from their environment, and in conditions of light different from those where they were originally placed. It looks like judging Shakespeare's plays from a dictionary of quotations.

[1] அரிவாள். [2] அரிவாள் மணை. [3] அச்சு [4] விமானம்.
கோபுரம். [6] ஆலாபனம். [7] ராகம்.

Indian art did not aim at producing specım ng room, but the æsthetic sense was correlated with o every object, big or small, was decorated with art work, the only undecorated objects being the head and neck of a widow who wants to observe life-long mourning. Hence our ladies love to decorate their persons with jewels and silks and it will be an unhappy day for India if their æsthetic sense is blunted by the modern virtue of possessing a bank-balance and they should sell their personal decorations, their 'barbaric pearl and gold' for developing the habit of depositing their wealth in banks. The Tamil ladies of ancient times were decorated in various ways. Their *kūndal*[1] was dressed in various artistic ways, one of which was in imitation of *suṟavu vāy*,[2] shark's mouth. Other ways of *mayirmudi*[3] or binding the hair into knots were *uchchi*,[4] *koṇḍai*,[5] *koppu*,[6] *sigaḷigai*,[7] *tammilam*,[8] and *muchchi*.[9] The different kinds of garlands with which the head and neck were adorned have already been referred to. The body was painted with pastes and powders of various kinds. The chief of the pastes were *manjal*,[10] turmeric or saffron made into a paste, *śandanakkuḻambu*[11] also called *tēyvai*,[12] *śāndu*,[13] *toyil*,[14] *toyyil*,[15] sandal paste mixed with various scents. The latter was spread on the chest, the mammæ and the abdomen and beautiful designs in line-drawing drawn thereon. A variety of paste for the hair was called *tagaram*.[16] On the paste was strewn powders of several kinds. One such was *poṟchuṇṇam*,[17] powdered gems, gold, sandal wood, and camphor.

The Tamils were exceedingly fond of decoration; so there are many words meaning to decorate, *e.g.*, *aṇi*,[18] *ār*,[19] *śūḍu*,[20] *puṇai*,[21] *pūṇ*,[22] *malai*,[23] *miḷai*,[24] *vēy*,[25] *milai*,[26] *ey*, *vari*.[27]

So, too, there are numerous words which mean an ornament, of which some are *aṇi*,[28] *aṇikalam*,[29] *āram*,[30] *iḻai*,[31] *nagai*,[32] *paṇi*,[33] *pūṇ*,[34] *mañju*,[35] *madāṇi*,[36] *vaḷḷi*.[37] The lobes of the ears were pierced to receive the *tōḍu*[38] or *kūḻai*;[39] poorer people wore the *ōlai*,[40] which was at first a bit of tender palmyra leaf, sometime coloured, rolled into a circle; then the same was made of gold plate rolled into various shapes, including the shapes of mythological monsters; the same, set with gems, became the ear-ornament of the rich, *tāḷuruvi*,[41] *kaḍukkan*,[42] *kaḍippam*,[43] *kuṇukku*,[44] *koṭṭai*,[45] *tūkkam*,[46] *toṅgal*,[47] *vedam*,[48] were other ear-ornaments. The jewel symbolic of a married woman was the *tāli*[49] now made of gold and of a peculiar shape. Probably the original *tāli* was made of the teeth or claws of the bear or the tiger[50] killed by the husband in the chase. It may be noted that

[1]Other names for the hair that adorns the head of ladies were ***aḷagam***, ***aimbāl*** ***ōdi***, ***kural***, ***kuruḷ***, ***kuḻal***, ***kūral***, ***kūḻai***, ***kōdai***, ***śuriyal***, ***śuruḷ***, ***neḍumai***, ***marāṭṭam***; that which grew equally plentifully on men's heads sometimes halfshorn, ***ilai***, ***ōri*** ***kuñji***, ***kuḍumi***, ***taḷai***, ***tongal***, ***navir***, ***pittai***; besides ***kaduppu***. ***kōli***, which meant both. கூந்தல், அளகம், ஐம்பால், ஓதி, குரல், குருள், குழல், கூரல், கூழல், கோதை, சுரியல், சுருள், நெடுமை, மராட்டம், இலை, ஓரி, குஞ்சி, குடுமி, தலை, தொங்கல், நவிர், பித்தை. கதுப்பு, கோலி.

[2]சுறவுவாய். [3]மயிர்முடி. [4]உச்சி. [5]கொண்டை. [6]கொப்பு. [7]சிகலிகை. [8]தம்மிலம். [9]முச்சி. [10]மஞ்சள். [11]சந்தனக்குழம்பு. [12]தேய்வை. [13]சாந்து. [14]தொயில். [15]தொய்யில். [16]தகரம். [17]பொற்சுண்ணம். [18]அணி. [19]ஆர். [20]சூடு. [21]புனை. [22]பூண். [23]மலை. [24]மிளை. [25]வேய். [26]மிலை. [27]வரி. [28]அணி. [29]அணிகலம். [30]ஆரம். [31]இழை. [32]நகை. [33]பணி. [34]பூண். [35]மஞ்சு. [36]மதாணி. [37]வள்ளி. [38]தோடு. [39]குழை. [40]ஓலை. [41]தாளுருவி. [42]கடுக்கன். [43]கடிப்பம். [44]குணுக்கு. [45]கொட்டை. [46]தூக்கம். [47]தொங்கல். [48]வேடம். [49]தாலி. [50]புலிப்பற்றாலி. *Kuṟundogai 161*.

South Indian women of all castes regard the *tāli* as the most sacred symbol of marriage, so much so that they will rather die than be without it for a second. But the tying of a *tāli* is not according to the Arya canon-law or North Indian practice an essential part of the wedding rite. According to the Arya law taking seven steps (*saptapati*) with the taking of the bride's hand (*pāṇigrahaṇam*) constitutes the act of marriage and if the bridegroom should die before the *saptapati* is completed, the woman does not become a widow and is fit for marrying another man. But this is not the belief of the women. What can be inferred from this ? Either the first Brāhmaṇas of South India were Tamil men affiliated to the Brāhmaṇa priesthood or, if they were all emigrants from North India, they took unto themselves Tamil women as their wives ; women being noted for their conservatism, the Tamil custom of tying a *tāli* as a symbol of marriage had to be given a premier place in the Brāhmaṇa wedding-rite. It is difficult to believe that, if the first Brāhmaṇa men and women were both foreign emigrants, they borrowed a Tamil custom and made it more important than their Ārya ones. Other important ornaments were strings of gold-thread, pearls, coral, etc., provided with pendants set with gems. They were called *kāḻ*,[1] *tāmam*,[2] *savi*,[3] *saraḍu*,[4] *koḍi*,[5] *nāṇ*,[6] *saṅgili*,[7] *kayil*,[8] *kaḍai*,[9] *kōvai*,[10] *toḍar*,[11] *kokkuvām*.[12] The pendants besides the *tāli*, were *kavaḍi*,[13] *sarappaḷi*,[14] etc. At the waist were also worn strings of gold or silver, *kuṟaṅguśeri*,[15] *kavānaṇi*,[16] *paṭṭigai*,[17] on which were strung little tinkling bells, *sadaṅgai*,[18] *kiṇkiṇi*.[19] Ornaments for the ankles were *śilambu*,[20] *kaḻal*,[21] *pāḍagam*.[22] They were also furnished with tinkling bells. At the wrists and above the elbows were worn *vaḷai*,[23] literally a circle, *kāppu*,[24] a guard, *kanṟu*,[25] *kurugu*,[26] *saṅgu*,[27] *śari*,[28] *śūḍagam*,[29] *toḍi*,[30] *vaṇḍu*,[31] *vaḷḷi*,[32] *piḍigam*.[33] Several forms of wristlets, bracelets and anklets were given by kings as a reward for feats of strength or skill. The fingers and toes were ornamented with rings, *mōdiram*,[34] *āḻipīli*.[35] Women wore a cap of pearls for the mammæ,[36] which were tied by means of a belt, *mulaikkachchu*[37]. Besides human beings, elephants, horses, bulls and even vehicles were heavily decorated.

Here is a description of a highly-decorated cot. 'They take the tusks of the fiercely-fighting elephant, which have dropped of their own accord, and cut the sides till they are of uniform shape and colour, fix between them leaves carved by the sharp chisels of the skilled carpenter. They place all round panels carved with scenes of lion-hunting and lined with many-coloured hairs of tigers; they decorate it with twigs, jasmin and other flowers ; they furnish the cot with windows. Then they hang all around the broad cot, curtains made of pearls strung on thread. They tie tapes woven with coloured lines so as to look like the stripes of a tiger. The ends of the legs of the cot are rounded like bowls which look like the breasts of a pregnant woman ; above the bowls, the legs are made to look like roots of

[1] காழ். [2] தாமம். [3] சவி. [4] சரடு. [5] கொடி. [6] நாண். [7] சங்கிலி. [8] கயில். [9] கடை. [10] கோவை. [11] தொடர். [12] கொக்குவாம். [13] கவடி. [14] சரப்பளி. [15] குறங்குசெறி. [16] கவானணி. [17] பட்டிகை. [18] சதங்கை. [19] கிண்கிணி. [20] சிலம்பு. [21] கழல். [22] பாடகம். [23] வளை. [24] காப்பு [25] கன்று. [26] குருகு [27] சங்கு. [28] சரி. [29] சூடகம். [30] தொடி. [31] வண்டு. [32] வள்ளி. [33] பிடிகம். [34] மோதிரம். [35] ஆழிபீலி. [36] முத்தணி கொங்கை *Tiruvāśagam* ix. 10–1 [37] மூலைக்கச்சு ஆரந்தாங்கிய அலர்முலை யாகத்து. *Neḍunelvāḍai 136.*

garlic. The bed, stitched thin and broad, was filled with the pure-coloured down of a swan in love; on it were placed pillows; on it was spread a sheet, woven with figures of the water-lily and well-starched.[1]

AMUSEMENTS

The ancient Tamils were a mirth loving people; they gave themselves up to merry-making frequently. Till Aryan religious ideas took firm root in their minds in the post-Christian centuries pessimism did not pull them down. They did not indulge in dark cogitations about the evils of earthly existence and seek for means to abolish the present joys of life for securing a future state of unchanging bliss. Their religious rites, *viḻavu*[2] were accompanied by drinking, singing, dancing and dumb show. Their secular amusements were the chase, *vēṭṭai*,[3] *āgēḍagam*[4], *pābatti*[5], wrestling, *marpor*[6], sword play, single stick, *śilambam*[7], racing with chariots, elephants, bulls, etc. *pandayam*,[8] playing with balls, *ammānai*[9], *pandu*[10], gambling and playing with shells, *kavaḍi*[11], *palagaṟai*[12], *alagu*[13], *sōḻi*[14]. Music was called *iśai*[15] or *pāṭṭu*[16], and has been partly discussed under war. Different kinds of tunes, *paṇ*,[17] one at least for each region, was developed. Probably the *paṇ* of *kuṟiñji* is the tune called *kuṟiñji* to-day. That of *mullai* was perhaps what is now called *madhyamāvatī*, for this is also called *brindāvana sāraṅga*. That of *marudam* was perhaps that called *kēdāram*, for *kēdāram*, like *marudam*, means a ploughed field. The *paṇ* for Neydal was probably that now called *punnāgavarāḷi*, that now used for sailor's songs. Instrumental music was called *pāṇ* and as bards accompanied their songs with playing on the *yāḻ*, they were called *pāṇar*. There were various forms of drums, the beating of which accompanied singing and dancing. Different kinds of measures or volleys were beaten for different occasions. As specimens, the following may be mentioned: *ēṟukoṭpaṟai*,[18] the cattle

[1] பொருதொழி நாக மொழியெயி றருகெறிந்து
சீருஞ் செம்மையு மொப்ப வல்லோன்
கூருளிக் குயின்ற வீரிலை யிடையிடுபு
தூங்கியன் மகளிர் வீங்குமுலை கடுப்பப்
புடைதிரண் டிருந்த குடத்த விடைதிரண்
டுள்ளி கோன்முதல் பொருத்தி யடியமைத்துப்
பேரள வெய்திய பெரும்பெயர்ப் பாண்டில்
மடைமா ணுண்ணிழை பொலியத் தொடைமாண்டு
குத்துடைச் சாலேக நாற்றிக் குத்தறுத்துப்
புலிப்பொறிக் கொண்ட பூங்கேழ்த் தட்டத்துத்
தகடுகண் புதையக் கொளீஇத் துகடீர்ந்
ஆட்டுறு பன்மயிர் விரைஇ வயமான்
வேட்டம் பொறித்து வியன்கட் கானத்து
முல்லைப் பலபோ துறழப் பூநிரைத்து
மெல்லிதின் விரிந்த சேக்கை மேம்படத்
துணைபுண ரன்னத் தூநிறத் தூவி
யிணையணை மேம்படப் பாயணை யிட்டுக்
காடிகொண்ட கழுவுறு கலிங்கத்துத்
தோடமைத் தூமடி விரித்த சேக்கை.

Neḍunalvāḍai 117–135.

[2] விழவு. [3] வேட்டை. [4] ஆகேடகம். [5] பாபத்தி. [6] மற்போர [7] சிலம்பம். [8] பந்தயம் [9] அம்மானை. [10] பந்து. [11] கவடி. [12] பலகறை. [3] அளகு. [14] சோழி. [15] இசை. [16] பாட்டு. [17] பண். [18] ஏறுகோட்பறை.

ting measure, *murugiyam*[1], measure for *veṛiyāṭṭam*[2], Muruga ınce, *maṇamuḷavu*[3], marriage drum, *nellarikiṇai*,[4] harvest drum, *rōṭṭupparai*[5], the drum beaten for dragging cars, *puṛappāṭṭup-ṛaṛai*,[6] the drum announcing the king's or a god's going out of the *kōil*, *mīnkōṭparai*[7], the drum beat announcing a haul of fish, *śūṛaikōṭparai*[8], dacoity-drum. Different kinds of noises were also emitted from trumpets to suit various occasions, auspicious and inauspicious, marriage or death processions.

Dancing, *āṭṭam*[9], *kūttu*[10], was of various kinds. Almost every incident of life had its appropriate dance. *Kūttu*, *kaḷi*[11], *kunippu*,[12] was a kind of dumb show, in which ideas were expressed by dancing and by elaborate gestures. This was the ancient form of the Tamil drama—the drama where the characters spoke or sang their parts belonged to North India—and is still kept up in Malabar under the name *kathakaḷi*[13]. *Kūttar*[14], *kaṇṇuḷar*[15], and *kūttiyar*[16] were elaborately made up. The actresses were women of easy virtue for *kūttiyar* has come to mean harlots. Children's dances were *kummi*[17], *teḷḷēṇam*[18], *sāḷal*[19], *ōrai*[20], etc. Boys played a kind of primitive cricket, in which the bat and the ball were both represented by long and short sticks, *kiṭṭu*[21], *puḷ*.[22]

Music was dispensed by wandering bards who were generally famished if they stuck to their homes.

'O *Pāṇan*, whose legs are tired by wandering from place to place like birds in search of fruits on hills which are covered by mist on the cessation of rain, because you have no one to support you in the world surrounded by the sea, and are surrounded by relatives crying for food, whose body is emaciated and whose mouth denounces the learning he has acquired'.[23]

Angling was another amusement. The following is a description of angling :—

'The expert angler of the *pāṇar* tribe carries on his shoulders a leather-bag full of bits of meat and sticks it at the end of a string tied to a long bamboo stick ; the fish bites the meat hanging at the bent end of the angling-rod and shakes the string ; missing it, the *vāḷai* fish stays with open mouth.'[24]

Capturing game by means of nets was another favourite amusement.

[1]முருகியம். [2]வெறியாட்டம் [3]மணமுழவு. [4]நெல்லரிகிணை. [5]தேரோட்டுப்பறை. [6]புறப்பாட்டுப்பறை. [7]மீன்கோட்பறை [8]சூறைகோட்பறை. [9]ஆட்டம். [10]கூத்து. [11]களி. [12]குனிப்பு. [13]கதகளி. [14]கூத்தர் [15]கண்ணுளர். [16]கூத்தியர். [17]கும்மி. [18]தெள்ளேணம். [19]சாழல். [20]ஓரை. [21]கிட்டு. [22]புள்.

[23]தண்கடல் வரைப்பிற் றுங்குநர் பெறாது
பொழிமழை துறந்த புகைவேல் குன்றத்துப்
பழுமரந் தேரும் பறவை போலக்
கல்லென் சுற்றமொடு கால்கிளர்ந்து திரிதரும்
புல்லென் யாக்கைப் புலவுவாய்ப் பாண.

Perumbāṇāṛṛuppaḍai, 18-22.

[24]பச்சூன் பெய்த சுவல்பிணி பைந்தோற்
கோள்வல் பாண்மகன் தலைவலித் தியாத்த
நெடுங்கழைத் தூண்டில் நடுங்க நாண்கொளீஇக்
கொடுவா யிரும்பின் மடிதலை புலம்பப்
பொதியிரை கதுவிய போழ்வாய் வாளை.

Perumbāṇāṛṛuppaḍai, 283-287.

'Hard-eyed hunters fix closely woven nets on the thorns of the hedges of fields in Pālaī land and drive into them rabbits which have long ears like the outer petals of the thorny-stalked lotus, they then proceed along with dogs whose jaws are wide-open, beat the shrubs and hunt the rabbit and eat them'.[1]

Trials of strength by wrestling was also a common amusement among the Tamils; the following is a description of *maṟpor*, wrestling[2] :—

In Āmūr which produces sweet and strong liquor he overcame the great strength of the wrestler; he bent one of his knees and planted it on his adversary's chest; with the other leg he defeated the tactics, bent the back of his rival; as an elephant which tries to eat a bamboo, he hammered his rival's head and feet and conquered him: may Tittan the heroic father of the wrestler see the sight, whether it would please him or not.

MEANS OF TRANSPORT

Walking was the only means of transport in nomad times. Modern anthropological opinion is coming round to the view that the Stone Age man was a great wanderer from the earliest times and that there was much intercourse between Asia and Africa on the one hand, and Europe and even America on the other, if not as much as there is in these days of the steam engine. The primitive nomad, hide-clad or skyclad, shouldered his tools and walked from country to country and spread the different stages of palæolithic culture all over the world. The motive for this travel was perhaps quest for food and the necessity for avoiding climatic rigour; or perhaps it was merely due to wanderlust and to the non-development of house building and of the habit of storing wealth, and living in one place to guard it from enemies. With the building of permanent habitations and the development of a love of luxury man began to make vehicles. The earliest kind of vehicle was the cart, *vaṇḍil*[3] also called *ūrdi*,[4] *oḻugai*[5], *śagaḍu*[6], *śādu*,[7] *vaiyam*.[8] *Vaṇḍil* now shortened into *vaṇḍi* literally means the bent place, from root of *vaḷ* to bend, whence *vaḷai*[9] to surround, to besiege,

[1] பகுவாய் ஞமலியொடு பைம்புத லெருக்கித்
தொகுவாய் வேலித் தொடர்வலை மாட்டி
முள்ளரைத் தாமரைப் புல்லிதழ் புரையு
நெடுஞ்செவிக் குறுமுயல் போக்கற வளைஇக்
கடுங்கட் கானவர் கடறு கூட்டுண்ணு
மருஞ்சுரம்.

Perumbāṇāṟṟuppaḍai, l.1-117.

[2] இன்கடுங் கள்ளி னாமூ ராங்கண்
மைந்துடை மல்லன் மதவலி முருக்கி
யொருகால் மார்பொதுங் கின்றே யொருகால்
வருதார் தாங்கிப் பின்னொதுங் கின்றே
நல்கினு நல்கா னாயினும் வெல்போர்ப்
போரருந் தித்தன் காண்கதி லம்ம
பசித்துப் பணைமுயலும் யானை போல
விருதலை யொசிய வெற்றிக்
களம்புகு மல்லற் கடந்தடு நிலையே.

Puṟam. 80

[3] வண்டில். [4] ஊர்தி. [5] ஒழுகை [6] சகடு. [7] சாடு. [8] வையம்.

to tie, and as a noun, a hole, also bangles, from their circular shape, a discus, a conch, *vaḷaiyam*[1] a tank, a hoop, *vaṭṭil*[2], a basket, a tray, a cup, *vaṭṭam*[3], a circle, a bull roarer, a shield, a tank, all named from the shape, *vaṭṭaṇai*[4], a circle, a cymbal, *vaṭṭu*[5], a spheroidal pawn used in gambling, *vaṇaṅgu*[6], to bow, to adore, *vaṇar*[7], an arched roof, *vaṇḍu*,[8] a beetle that wheels round and round, *vaḷi*[9], whirlwind, *vaḷḷam*[10], a round eating tray, *vaḷḷi*[11], a bracelet. From early times the people were familiar with a cart and named its various parts. *Achchu*[12], the axle tree, *āṇi*[13] (a word found also in the *Rig Veda*), *iruśu*,[14] *kandu*[15], axle pin, *uruḷai*[16], *uṇḍai*[17], *kāl*[18], wheel, *ār*[19], spokes *śūḍu*[20], tyre, *kuṟaḍu*[21] hub, etc. All parts of the cart were heavily carved.[22] The carts were used more for purposes of trade than for travel. Kings and noblemen used a *tēr*, car, as already described. The main streets of a city and the roads intended for travel by royal cars were broad. The cars were dragged by bulls, elephants, and in later times by horses. Kings and noblemen also travelled in palanquins, *pallakku*[23], *aṇigam*[24], *taṇḍigai*[25]; those with gems embedded on them were called *kañjigai*[26]. Transport on water was by means of boats of several kinds and made in several ways, *kappal*[27], *ōḍam*[28], *ambi*[29], *tōṇi*[30], *teppam*[31], *pariśal*[32], *paḍagu*[33], *kalam*[34], *uḍubam*[35], *kōlam*[36], *toḷḷam*[37], *pagaḍu*[38], *paḍuvai*[39], *paṭṭi*[40], *puruvai*[41], *puṇai*[42], *midavai*[43], *vaḷḷam*[44], *timil*[45]. It needs scarcely be added that the heads of boats were carved in the shape of the face of lions, elephants, horses, etc., and they were called in later times *arimugavambi*[46], *karimugavambi*[47], *kudiraimugavambi*[48] respectively. Boats were made in several ways; thus *teppam* was a float made of logs bound together, *timil*, a catamaran for fishing, *tōṇi*, a wicker work construction covered with hide, *valam*, a dugout, *paḍagu*, *kappal*, sailing boats and *ōḍam*, one rowed with oars. Sailing boats were furnished with *kūmbu*[49], mast and *pāy*[50], *idai*[51], sails.

Many words were used to indicate a ship: *ambi*,[52] *ōṅgal*,[53] *kalam*,[54] *śadā*,[55] *śōṅgu*,[56] *timil*.[57] *toḷḷai*,[58] *tōṇi*,[59] *navvu*,[60] *pāḥri*,[61] *pādai*,[62] *pāradi*[63], *pāṟu*[64], *puṇai*[65], *pōdam*[66], *madalai*[67], *vaṅgam*,[68] *poṟi*[69]. The Tamils ought to have been very familiar with boats and ships and to have constantly used them for purposes of transport by water, before they were prompted to invent nearly twenty names for it. The eastern and western coast lines were in olden days dotted with numerous ports, many of which have become useless on account of the retreat of the sea and almost all of which have become deserted by the modern developments of commercial intercourse by sea.

[1] வளையம். [2] வட்டில். [3] வட்டம். [4] வட்டணை. [5] வட்டு. [6] வணங்கு. [7] வணர். [8] வண்டு. [9] வளி. [10] வள்ளம். [11] வள்ளி. [12] அச்சு. [13] ஆணி. [14] இருசு. [15] கந்து. [16] உருளை. [17] உண்டை. [18] கால். [19] ஆர். [20] சூடு. [21] குறடு.

[22] கூருளி பொருத வடிவாழ் நோன்குறட்
டாரஞ் சூழ்ந்த வயில்வாய் நேமி

Siṟupāṇāṟṟupaḍai, 252–253.

The wheel whose tyre went round felloes inserted in a hub on which figures were carved with a sharp chisel,

[23] பல்லக்கு. [24] அணிகம். [25] தண்டிகை. [26] கஞ்சிகை. [27] கப்பல். [28] ஓடம். [29] அம்பி. [30] தோணி. [31] தெப்பம். [32] பரிசல். [33] படகு. [34] கலம். [35] உடுபம். [36] கோலம். [37] தொள்ளம். [38] பகடு. [39] படுவை. [40] பட்டி. [41] புருவை. [42] புணை. [43] மிதவை. [44] வள்ளம். [45] திமில். [46] அரிமுகவம்பி. [47] கரிமுகவம்பி. [48] குதிரைமுகவம்பி. [49] கூம்பு. [50] பாய். [51] இதை. [52] அம்பி. [53] ஓங்கல். [54] கலம். [55] சதா. [56] சோங்கு. [57] திமில். [58] தொள்ளை. [59] தோணி [60] நவ்வு. [61] பஃறி. [62] பாதை. [63] பாரதி. [64] [illegible] [65] புணை. [66] போதம். [67] மதலை. [68] வங்கம். [69] பொறி.

Food

Before discussing the food habits of the ancient Tamils it may be pointed out that Indians, throughout the ages, have been mainly vegetarians. Not that they did not love the taste of meat; on the contrary when they got it they ate it with great delight.[1] Nor did they throw to the dogs the game they hunted, without consuming it themselves. But Indians never made the flesh of animals their staple food like the people of Western Europe. The latter living in countries where cereals cannot be produced in abundance, have been forced by their environment to adopt meat as their chief article of food and add to their dietary a minimum quantity of vegetable substance, because meat by itself is not a perfect food and because they cannot resist nature's urge to consume vegetable products charged with the chlorides, and iodides, the sulphates and phosphates and other salts necessary for the healthy life of a body. To use Indian phraseology, meat is their food and vegetable their curry; that is they eat meat to sustain their bodies and cereals and other vegetarian food to add relish to their meat. In India the position is reversed. Rice, wheat, the millets and the pulses are our food, and meat (and green-vegetables) our curry; that is we eat rice or wheat or millet and the seeds of legumes to rebuilid tissue lost by combustion, and meat and green vegetables turned into curry to add relish to the cereals which are mostly insipid in themselves and unfitted to stimulate to activity the glands which secrete saliva and other juices necessary for dissolving and digesting starches and proteids. In other words meat is food to Europeans and but curry to Indians. In this connection I may point out that curry, *karī*[2], is the name in Tamil not only of curried meat or vegetable and of sauce in general, but also

[1] A bard thus describes how he gobbled meat when he was plied with it by a royal patron :

துராஅய் துற்றிய துருவையம் புழுக்கின்
பராரை வேவை பருகெனத் தண்டிக்
காழிற் சுட்ட கோழூன் கொழுங்குறை
ஊழி னூழின் வாய்வெய் தொற்றி
யவையவை முனிகுவ மெனினே சுவைய

Porunarāṟṟuppaḍai, 103-107.

'He urged me many times to eat the stout, well boiled loin of a ram fed with bundles of arugu grass (*Agrostis Linearis*). I ate big lumps of fat flesh, roasted at the end of iron spikes, and, as they were hot, shifted them from the right side of the mouth to the left to cool them. I then said we did not require any more boiled or roasted meat.' And again—

கொல்லை யுழுகொழு வேய்ப்பப் பல்லே
யெல்லையு மிரவு மூன்றின் றழுங்கி
யுயிர்ப்பிடம் பெறாஅ தூண்முனிந்து

Ibid., 117-119.

'Our teeth, on account of eating meat night and day, became blunt like the blade (plough-share) of the plough with which the garden in the back yard is ploughed, and having no place for rest got disgusted with food. And again—

பால்வறைக் கருனை காடியின் மிதப்ப
வயின்ற காலை

Ibid., 115-116.

'When I swallowed milk and fried meat till I was filled to the neck.'

means black pepper. This proves that in old times meat and vegetables were boiled with black pepper to turn into curry. In passing I may remark that chiliy, *capsicum*, now universally used as a substitute for black pepper in Indian cookery, is a thing introduced into this country from Chili in South America, in recent times, that is, after the rise of modern European trade with India. Hence it has no *iḍukuṛi*[1] names as has black pepper, i.e., *miriyal*[2], *miḷagu*[3], *kaṛi*[4], *kalinai*[5], *kāyam*[6], *tiraṅgal*[7], but merely a *kāraṇappeyar*[8], viz., *miḷagukāy*[9], the fruit that produces a substance like pepper, in Telugu, *miryiapukāya*, the *miriyam*—fruit. Europeans imported pepper from old India from before the Christian Era, their tongues having been captivated by its biting taste or rather touch, for it is touch nerves and not taste nerves that are titillated by the bite of pepper ; hence Sanskrit has a *kāraṇapeyar*, *yoga*—name for pepper, namely *yavanapriyā*, dear to the *yavana*, i.e., the Greeks and the Romans. Though the ancient *yavanas* carried pepper from India in their ships they made a mess of its name, for they did not borrow for it its proper name of *kaṛi*, or *miriyal* or *miḷagu*, but called it *pippali* (whence *pepperos*, pepper) which is the name of long pepper[10]. In the middle ages Western Europe imported pepper from India, not for eating, but for sprinkling its powder on meat before drying it for use as food in wintry weather. Such meat was called 'powdered meat'. Thus pepper was a luxury in ancient Europe and a necessity in mediæval Europe ; Venetian bottoms, at first, and later Dutch ones, carried pepper to Western Europe and it was because the avaricious merchants of Holland doubled the price of pepper at the end of the sixteenth century, that in 1599 the East India Company was started, the final result of which was the development of the British Empire in India.

To return to the ancient Tamils. They ate meat, the various names of which *ūn*[11], *iṛaichchi*[12], *pulāl*[13], *tunnu*[14], *ūttai*[15], *ūḷttal*[16], *taśai*,[17] *taḍi*[18], *tūvu*[19], *puṉ*[20], *puraṇi*[21], *pulavu*[22], *vallūram*[23], *viḍakku*[24], indicate their fondness for it, as curry and not as food, just as their modern descendants do. This curry was of various kinds (1) *kuy*[25], *tāḷitta kari*[26], sprinkled with pepper powder, mustard, etc., fried in oil ; (2) *karunai*[27], *porikkaṛi*[28], *varai*[29], *tuvaṭṭaṛkaṛi*[30], fried meat ; (3) *tuvai*[31], *puḷiṅgaṛi*[32], meat boiled with tamarind and pepper. While on the subject of *kaṛi* I may mention also *kāḍi*[33], *ūṛukaṛi*[34], pickles, fruits soaked in oil or water with flavouring substances.[35]

The Aryas of North India were as great lovers of meat as were the Tamils of South India. From the evidence of the Vedic mantras we

[2]மிரியல். [3]மிளகு. [4]கறி. [5]கலினை. [6]காயம். [7]திரங்கல். [8]காரணப்பெயர். [9]மிளகுகாய். [10]திப்பிலி. [11]ஊன். [12]இறைச்சி. It is noteworthy that the word also means, that which is agreeable. [13]புலால். [14]துன்னு. [15]ஊத்தை. [16]ஊழ்த்தல். [17]தசை. [18]தடி. [19]தூவு. [20]புன். [21]புரணி. [22]புலவு. [23]வல்லூரம். [24]விடக்கு. [25]குய். [26]தாளித்த கறி. [27]கருனை. [28]பொரிக்கறி. [29]வறை. [30]துவட்டற்கறி. [31]துவை. [32]புளிங்கறி [33]காடி. [34]ஊறுகறி.

[35]பைந்துணர்

நெடுமரக் கொக்கி னறுவடி விதிர்த்த
தகைமாண் காடி

Perumbāṇaṛṛuppaḍai, 308–310

The sweet-smelling tender clustered fruit of the mango, preserved.

learn that 'horses',[1], 'bulls'[2], 'buffaloes'[3], 'rams'[4], and 'goats'[5] were killed on slaughter-benches, *sūnā*,[6], cooked in caldrons,[7] and eaten. The eating of fishes and birds must have also prevailed because fishing and bird-catching are referred to.[8] In North India there was developed a prejudice against eating the village-fowl, because it feeds on all kinds of repulsive offal; such a prejudice does not seem to have ever risen in South India. In early times there was no sentiment against beef-eating in North India. In the later Vedic age the objection to the eating the flesh of the bull and the cow first arose. Says the *Satapatha Brāhmaṇa*, 'Let him not eat (the flesh) of either the cow or the ox; for the cow and the ox doubtless support everything here on earth. The Gods spake, 'verily the cow and the ox support everything here: Come, let us bestow on the cow and the ox whatever belongs to other species; accordingly they bestowed on the cow and the ox whatever vigour belonged to other species of animals; and therefore the cow and the ox eat most. Hence were one to eat the flesh of an ox or of a cow, there would be as it were an eating of everything, or as it were a going on to the end or to destruction. Such a one indeed would be likely to be born again as a strange being (as one of whom there is) evil report, such as he has expelled an embryo from a woman, he has committed a sin; let him therefore not eat the flesh of the cow and the ox. Nevertheless Yājñavalkya said, 'I for one eat it, provided that it is tender.'[9] Yājñavalkya Rishi, who probably belonged to the early years of the first millennium B.C. was not frightened by the threat that the eating of beef was tantamount to the dreaded sin of *brūṇahatti*; hence the virulent disgust at the very idea of beef-eating that is the marked characteristic of the Hindus to-day is less than of three thousand years' standing. South Indians too of ancient times did not seem to have had much objection to eat the flesh of the cow. As was the case with all other things they liked, they had several names for beef, viz., *vaḷḷūram*[10], *śuṭṭiṛaichchi*[11], *śūśiyam*[12], *paḍittiram*.[13] In later times the objection to beef-eating became violent all through India except among the depressed classes, whose social degradation made them so poor and so incapable of earning enough food that they had no objection to meat of any kind—the flesh of the cow or the buffalo and even the flesh of animals that have died on account of disease. Among the other classes the sentiment against beef-eating developed primarily on account of economical causes. The above is plainly indicated by the remark in the passage from the *Satapatha Brāhmaṇa* that 'were one to eat the flesh of an ox or a cow, there would be as it were, a going on to the end or to destruction'; besides the need of cattle for agriculture, other reasons were the wide use of milk and milk products in Indian dietary and the moral reason, i.e., the love inspired by the meek and gentle-eyed cow.

The chief cereal used by the Tamils was the paddy *nel*[14], *vari*[15], the names of various varieties of which existed, such as *śeñjāli*[16], *śennel*[17],

[1] A.V. vi. 71, 1. [2] R. V. i. 164. 43. [3] R.V. v. 29. 7. [4] R.V., x. 27. 17.
[5] A.V. i. 162–3. [6] R.V. x. 86. 18. [7] R.V. iii. 53. 22.
[8] P. T. Srinivasa Iyengar, *Life in Ancient India*, p. 49.
[9] *S.B.* iii 1. 2. 21, Eggeling's Translation, ii, p. 11. [10] வள்ளூரம்.
[11] சுட்டிறைச்சி. [12] சூசியம். [13] படித்திரம். [14] நெல். [15] வரி. [16] செஞ்சாலி. [17] செந்நெல்.

sol[1], *iyavai*[2], *aivanam* ;[3] paddy three years old and very healthy eating, *aśam*[4] ; *pongaḷi*[5], was paddy not dusted. Ordinarily paddy was boiled before it was husked ; this was called *puḷuṅgalariśi*[6], and as the health-giving vitamins and the muscle-building rice germs are best preserved in this form of rice, it was most widely eaten. Raw rice was called *pachchaiariśi*[7]. Well pounded rice cleaned well of bran was called *kuttalariśi*[8], or *avaiyal*[9] and one not very well cleaned was *koḻiyalariśi*[10]. The chief way of cooking rice was to boil it in water. As boiled rice was the principal food it had very many names, *adiśil*[11], *amalai*[12], *amudu*[13], *ayini*[14], *avi*[15], *aviḻ*[16], *aḷuppu*[17], *uṇā*[18], *uṇḍi*[19], *ūṇ*[20], *kūḻ*[21], *śadi*[22], *śādam*[23], *śoṉṟi*[24], *śōṟu*[25], *tuppu*[26], *tōri*[27], *parukkai*[28], *pāttu*[29], *piśi*[30], *pugarvu*[31], *puḻukkal*[32], *puṟkai*[33], *pommal*[34], *porugu*[35], *maḍai*[36], *miśai*[37], *midavai*[38], *mūral*[39], *valśi*[40].

Rice boiled along with pulses was called *poṅgal*[41]. The human palate insistently demands variety in the matter of cooking : other preparations of rice to meet this demand were *kaḷi*[42], *kūḻ*[43], *tulavai*[44], different forms of porridge, *kañji*[45], gruel, *nīrāram*[46], rice-water, *tōśai*[47], *aḍai*[48], different forms of rice-bread. *Poṟi*[49] parched rice, was another favourite food. Cakes were called *viragu*[50] or *paṇiyōram*[51], such as *appam*[52], *piṭṭu*[53], *akkulli*[54], *aṇḍagai*[55], *ilaiyaḍai*[56], *nolai*[57], *mellaḍai*[58], *pollal*[59], *poli*[60], *maṇḍigai*[61] *iḍi*[62], *saḥkulli*[63], *nuvaṇai*[64], *ochchai*[65], *tuvai*[66], *sīḍai*[67], *vaḍai*[68]. For some of these other grains than rice, such as *uḷundu*[69], *eḷ*[70], and many pulses were also used.

The grains eaten varied from region to region. Thus *varagu*[71], *Paspalum frumentaceum*, *śāmai*[72], panicum, *mudirai*[73], beans and lentils, were eaten in Mullai ; the mountain-rice called *aivanam*[74], *tinai*[75], *Panicum italicum*, *mūṅgilariśi*[76], bamboo rice, in Kuriñji ; *śennel*[77] and *veṇṇel*,[78] red rice and white rice, in Marudam ; in Pālai they ate whatever they could get by pillage and in Neydal, whatever they could barter for fish and salt.

Other things eaten were honey, *tēn*[79], which was also called *naṟavu*[80] *naṟai*[81], *piḻi*[82], *maṭṭu*[83], *tādu*[84], *pāgu*[85] chiefly eaten in Kuṟiñji,

[1] சொல். [2] இயவை. [3] ஐவனம். [4] அசம் [illegible] [6] புழுங்கலரிசி. [7] பச்சையரிசி.
[8] குத்தலரிசி. [9] அவையல். [10] கொழியலரிசி. [11] அடிசில். [12] அமலை. [13] அமுது. [14] அயினி.
[15] அவி. [16] அவிழ். [17] அழுப்பு. [18] உணா. [19] உண்டி. [20] ஊண். [2]. [22] [illegible] [23] சாதம்
[24] சொன்றி. [25] சோறு [26] துப்பு. [27] தோரி. [28] பருக்கை [illegible] பாத்து. [30] பிசி. [31] புகர்வு.
[32] புழுக்கல். [33] புற்கை. [34] பொம்மல். [35] பொருகு. [illegible] மடை. [37] மிசை. [38] மிதவை.
[39] மூரல். [40] வல்சி.

முகிழ்த்தகை
முரவை போகிய முரியா அரிசி
விரலென நிமிர்ந்த நிரலமை புழுக்கல்.

Porunarāṟṟuppaḍai, 112-14.

Rice grains, whole and unbroken, without lines on its surface like the tender buds of the mullai, *Jasminum trichotumum*, cooked so that each grain looked like a finger and was not sticking to the other grains. Cakes made of rice are thus described.

சுவைய
வேறுபல் உருவின் விரகு.

Ibid. 107-8.

Sweet cakes skilfully made of variegated shapes.

[41] பொங்கல். [42] களி. [43] கூழ். [44] துழவை. [45] கஞ்சி. [46] நீராரம். [47] தோசை. [48] அடை.
[49] பொரி [50] விரகு. [51] பணியாரம். [52] அப்பம். [53] பிட்டு. [54] அக்குல்லி. [55] அண்டகை.
[56] இலையடை [57] நொலை. [58] மெல்லடை. [59] பொல்லல். [60] போலி. [61] மண்டிகை. [62] இடி.
[63] சஃகுல்லி. [64] நுவணை. [65] ஒச்சை. [66] துவை. [67] சீடை. [68] வடை. [69] உளுந்து. [70] எள்.
[71] வரகு. [72] சாமை. [73] முதிரை [74] ஐவனம். [75] தினை. [76] மூங்கிலரிசி. [77] செந்நெல்.
[78] வெண்ணெல். [79] தேன். [80] நறவு [81] நறை. [2] பிழி. [83] மட்டு. [84] தாது. [5] பாகு.

tēn and *tinai ma*[1] being a favourite combination; *vellam*[2], *akkāram*[3] jaggery, was substituted for honey in Marudam, sugar was not freely used, it being originally a product imported from China; there is no *idukuṟi* name for it in Sanskrit or Tamil; Sanskrit *sarkkarā* (whence European names of sugar are derived) as well as Tamil *ayir*,[4] sugar, originally meant sand and were, by metonymy, extended to jaggery refined into a powdery form. Jaggery was manufactured by boiling down the juice of the sugar-cane, *karumbu*[5], also called *kaḻai*[6], *kannal*[7], *vēḻal*[8], to molasses, *tēṟal*[9], *tēnpāgu*[10], *kuḻambu*[11], *āṇam*,[12] and cooled in pots or wooden moulds, *achchu*.

Milk and milk products were used largely. The chief milk products were *ēḍu*[13], cream, *ṭayir*[14], *perugu*[15], *musaru*[16], curdled milk, *mōr*[17], *arumbam*[18], *aḷai*[19], *machchigai*[20], *muśar*[21], curdled milk from which butter has been churned out, *veṇṇey*[22], *veṇkaṭṭi*[23], butter, and *ney*[24], ghi. It is curious that though ghi is clarified butter, the name for the latter is derived from the former, for *veṇṇey* is but white ghi. The cause of this order of naming the original article from the derived one is not quite clear; probably as butter cannot keep without getting rancid in tropical climates, it was never stored, but immediately after it was churned out, it was turned into ghi and the necessity for a name for the intermediate product was not felt for a long time.

That in the matter of food Aryan India and Tamil India had absolutely the same customs is proved by the fact that meat of all kinds was eaten both in the North and the South and by the following account of Arya food, other than meat. 'Of the animal food derived from the living animal, milk[25] sometimes mixed with honey[26] brought by toiling bees[27], ghi[28], butter[29] and curds[30] were consumed. Yava is frequently mentioned in the sense of corn in general or barley. (Wheat and barley were the grains used by the Aryas in addition to the South Indian ones). Rice, barley, beans and sesamum were the chief vegetable foodstuffs of the day.[31] Grain was eaten parched[32] and made into cakes[33] or boiled in water[34] or in milk.[35] Meal boiled with curd into Karambha[36] and gruel,[37] i.e., parched meal boiled in milk were other forms of food. . . . As now hot freshly cooked food was preferred[38] to cold food. Fruits were also eaten.[39] Food was served on leaf-platters,[40] the lotus leaf being commonly used for the purpose. Skins filled with honey[41] or curds, jars[42] of honey,[43] rice husked by servant-girls[44] and stored in earthern vessels[45] and flour obtained by grinding corn in mill stones,[46] were stocked in houses.[47] This shows that the difference between Arya and Dasyu was neither racial nor cultural but only one of cult.

[1] தேனுந் தினைமாவும். [2] வெல்லம். [3] அக்காரம். [4] அயிர். [5] கரும்பு. [6] கழை. [7] கன்னல். [8] வேழம். [9] தேறல். [10] தேன்பாகு. [11] குழம்பு. [12] ஆணம். [13] ஏடு. [14] தயிர். [15] பெருகு. [16] முசரு. [17] மோர். [18] அரும்பம். [19] அளை. [20] மச்சிகை. [21] முசர். [22] வெண்ணெய். [23] வெண்கட்டி. [24] நெய்.

[25] R. V. x. 49, 10. [26] R. V. viii. 4, 8. [27] R. V. x. 106, 9.
[28] R. V. iv. 58. [29] Sarpis, A. V. ix. 6, 41. [30] R. V. vi. 57, 2.
[31] A. V. vi. 140, 4. [32] *Dhānā*, R. V. iii. 35, 3.
[33] *Apūpam*, R. V. iii. 52, 7; *Puroḍāsam*, A. V. xii. 4, 35.
[34] *Odanam*, A. V. iii. 34, 35. [35] R. V. viii. 66, 10. [36] A. V. iv. 7, 2.
[37] *Mantha*, A. V. x. 6, 2. [38] R. V. x. 79, 3. [39] R. V. i. 90, 8.
[40] A. V. viii. 10, 27. [41] R. V. iv. 45, 3, 4. [42] R. V. vi. 49, 18.
[43] R. V. i. 117, 6. [44] A. V. xii. 3, 13.
[45] A. V. vi. 142, 1. [46] *Drishat*, A. V. ii. 31, 1.
[47] P. T. Srinivas Iyengar, *Life in Ancient India*, p. 49.

One result of the extensive use of vegetables in food was that there are distinct words for the different stages of the edible parts of plants e.g., *piñju*,[1] *elu*,[2] *vaḍu*,[3] the very tender fruit, *kāy*,[4] *tīyaḷi*,[5] *palan*,[6] (which last word, I think, is pure Tamil, having nothing to do with Sanskrit *phalam*), the grown fruit, *kani*,[7] *paḻam*,[8] the fully ripened fruit, *śuḷai*,[9] pulp or edible part of a fruit, *taṇḍu*,[10] tender stem, also petal, *taḷir*,[11] tender leaf, *ilai*,[12] mature leaf; but the word for *kiḻangu*,[13] an esculent root, a tuber, has only synonyms borrowed from Sanskrit, e.g., *kandam*, *mūlam*; it has another synonym, *śakunam*, whose origin I cannot suggest; perhaps *vēr*,[14] root, and its Tamil synonyms *śaḍai*,[15] *śivai*,[16] and *tūr*[17] may also refer to tubers.

The ancient Tamils drank hard; liquor has more 'pure' Tamil names than any other article. Here are some of them; *ammiyam*,[18] *ari*,[19] *arugi*,[20] *aruppam*,[21] *aḷi*,[22] *aṛivaḷi*,[23] *āmbal*,[24] *āli*,[25] *ālai*,[26] *īḻam*,[27] *eli*,[28] *kalliyam*,[29] *kavvai*[30] *kaḷi*,[31] *kāli*,[32] *kuḍu*,[33] *kundi*,[34] *kongu*,[35] *śādi*,[36] *śāli*,[37] *śāṛu*,[38] *śikkar*,[39] *śuṇḍi*,[40] *śurai*,[41] *śūḷigai*,[42] *śēṛu*,[43] *śol*,[44] *śolviḷambi*,[45] *ñaḷi*,[46] *taṇiyal*,[47] *tumbi*,[48] *tēm*,[49] *tēṛal*,[50] *tēn*,[51] *toṇḍi*,[52] *tōppi*[53] (special name of rice-liquor), *naṛavu*,[54] *nanai*,[55] *nāṛṛam*,[56] *paḍu*,[57] *pāli*,[58] *piḻi*,[59] *pēdai*,[60] *maṭṭu*,[61] *madurai*,[62] *maruṭṭam*,[63] *marali*,[64] *māri*,[65] *māli*,[66] *murugu*,[67] *mēdai*,[68] *vaḍi*,[69] *viśuḷi*,[70] *veṛi*,[71] *vēri*;[72] *kaḷ*,[73] the vendors of liquor were called *śavuṇḍiyar*,[74] *tuvaśar*,[75] *paḍuvar*,[76] *paḻaiyar*,[77] *piḻiyar*.[78]

The following describes the food of the mountain-dwelling *Kuṛavar* and their hospitality.

'They mix the fat meat of the wild boar and venison cut from deer, killed when they were running, the flesh wounded by the bite of bitches; they fill themselves with the liquor brewed from honey and matured in bamboo cylinders and also with rice-liquor and they are full of glee. To bring down the intoxication due to drinking in the mornings, they mix pounded white nuts of the Jack fruit which have come down floating on rivers, have become over-ripe and burst out, with butter-milk to which has been added the sweet-sour tamarind fruit whose rind is white, and in this juice cook white rice matured in bamboo tubes, so that the smell of the boiling rice spreads all along the hill-side; you can get this food from the hands of the Kuṛava girls, who have black hair-knots smelling of flowers. They will offer you this food with great joy for having got a guest to feed; they will then introduce their children to you and will offer you besides the

[1] பிஞ்சு. [2] எழு. [3] வடு. [5] தீயளி. [6] பல
[7] கனி. [8] பழம். [9] சுளை. [11] தளிர்.
[13] கிழங்கு. [14] வேர். [15] சடை. [16] சிவை. [17] தூர். [18] அம்மியம்.
[19] அரி. [20] அருகி. [21] அருப்பம். [22] அளி. [23] அறிவழி. [24] ஆம்பல்.
[25] ஆலி. [26] ஆலை. [27] ஈழம். [28] எலி. [29] கல்லியம். [30] கவ்வை.
[31] களி. [32] காலி. [33] குடு. [34] குந்தி. [35] கொங்கு. [36] சாதி.
[37] சாலி. [38] சாறு. [39] சிக்கர். [40] சுண்டி. [41] சுரை.
[43] சேறு. [44] சொல். [45] சொல்விளம்பி [46] ஞாளி. [47] தணியல் [48] தும்பி.
[49] தேம் [50] தேறல். [51] தேன். [52] தொண்டி. [53] தொப்பி. [54] நறவு.
[55] நனை. [56] நாற்றம். [57] படு. [58] பாலி. [59] பிழி. [60] பேதை.
[61] மட்டு. [62] மதுரை. [63] மருட்டம். [64] மறலி. [65] மாரி. [66] மாலி.
[67] முருகு. [68] மேதை. [69] வடி. [70] விசுளி. [71] வெறி. [72] வேரி.
[73] கள். [74] சவுண்டியர். [75] துவசர். [76] படுவர். [77] பழையர் [78] பிழியர்.

products of the tops of hills (such as sandal, *agil*, gold, gems, etc.)'.[1] Of the hunters it is said:

'They drink the sweet rice-liquor, *tōppi*, brewed in their houses; they cut in the open field the strong bull and eat its meat. The drum faced with folded hides sounds and they lift the left arm, strong with the constant bending of the bow, place it around the right side and dance all day with glee.'[2]

The food of the *Āyar* is thus described:—

'Early in the morning when the thick darkness begins to disappear and birds rise from their sleep, *Iḍaiyar* women ply with the rope the churning-rod, *mattu*,[3] with a noise like the grunt of a tiger; they churn the milk with folded crust, having been curdled by the curds reserved for the purpose, *uṛai*,[4] which looks like the white mushroom, and remove the butter; they place a pad of flowers, *śummāḍu*[5], on their heads and stand thereon a pot of buttermilk, whose mouth is sprinkled with drops of curds and sell it in the mornings. They are dark of skin; at their ears dangle earrings; their shoulders are like the bamboo; their hair is short and wavy. They feast their relatives with rice bartered for buttermilk. Then they sell ghi and buy gold and milch buffaloes and cows and calves. If you stay with the *Iḍaiyar* with hanging lips, they will feast you with *tinai*,[6] which looks like the young of crabs, boiled with milk. Their strong feet are scarred with constant wearings of sandals; their hands lean on sticks with which they cruelly beat the cattle; and are horny with handling the axes which fell trees; their shoulders, scarred and hairy by carrying *Kāvaḍis*[7] with double hanging loops; their hair, smelling because they wipe the head with hands full of milk-drops. They wear garlands of mixed flowers, *Kalambagam*,[8] plucked from trees and plants growing in the forests;

[1] எறித் தரூஉ மிலங்குமலைத் தாரமொடு
வேய்ப்பெயல் விளையுட் டேக்கட் டேறல்
குறைவின்றி பருகி நறவுமகிழ்ந்து வைகறைப்
பழஞ்செருக் குற்றநும் மனந்தர் தீர
வருவி தந்த பழஞ்சிதை வெண்காழ்
வருவிசை தவிர்த்த கடமான் கொழுங்குறை
முளவுமாத் தொலைச்சிய பைந்நிணப் பிளவை
பிணவுநாய் முடுக்கிய தடியொடு விரைஇ
வெண்புடைக் கொண்ட துய்த்தலைப் பழனி
னின்புளிக் கலந்து மாமோ ராகக்
கழைவளர் நெல்லி னரியுலை யூழ்த்து
வழையமை சாரல் கமழத் துழைஇ
நறுமல ரணிந்த நாறிரு முச்சிக்
குறமக ளாக்கிய வாலவிழ் வல்சி
யகமலி யுவகை யார்வமொ டளைஇ
மகமுறை தடுப்ப மனைதொறும் பெறுகுவிர்.

Malaipaḍukaḍām, 170–185.

[2] இல்லடு கள்ளின் றோப்பி பருகி
மல்லன் மன்றத்து மதவிடை கெண்டி
மடிவாய்த் தண்ணுமை நடுவட் சிலைப்பச்
சிலைநவி லெறுழ்த்தோ ளோச்சி வலன்வளையூஉப்
பகன் மகிழ் தூங்கும்.

Perumbāṇāṟṟuppaḍai, 142–146.

[3] மத்து. [4] உறை. [5] சும்மாடு. [6] தினை.

they wear a single cloth which fits closely with the body, and eat porridge.[1]

The food of *marudam* is thus described :—

'The *śuḷai*[2] (pulp) of the Jack-fruit, sweet and fragrant, the fruits of the mango of many forms, and beautiful *kāy*[3] (unripe fruit) of numerous shapes, (like the plantain, the *pāgal*[4], and the brinjal), other fruits, (like the plantain and the cashew), leaf-curries of leaves, curled, thin, beautiful, growing on creepers which grow abundantly in the rainy season, crystals of sugar made from boiled sugar, and meat cooked together with big tubers which grow down and rice boiled in milk, sweet to eat, were served.'[5]

Fire for cooking and other purposes was made by churning wood.

The forester made fire by churning one piece of wood on another, as he does even to-day in forests remote from places where matches are sold. This is referred to in 'the fire which he churned,'[6] 'the lamp lighted from a fire, churned by hunters with dry wood brought by elephants.'[7] In the plains, they kept up a perpetual fire in fire-pots,

[1] நள்ளிருள் விடியற் புள்ளெழப் போகிப்
புலிக்குரன் மத்த மொலிப்ப வாங்கி
யாம்பி வான்முகி ழன்ன கூம்புமுகை
புறையமை தீர்ந்தயிர் கலக்கி நுரைதெரிந்து
புகர்வாய்க் குழிசி பூஞ்சுமட் டிரீஇ
நாண்மோர் மாறு நன்மா மேனிச்
சிறுகுழை துயல்வரும் காதிற் பணைத்தோட்
குறுநெறிக் கொண்ட கூந்த லாய்மக
ளளைவிலை யுணவிற் கிளையுட னருத்தி
நெய்விலைக் கட்டிப் பசும்பொன் கொள்ளா
ளெருமை நல்லான் கருநாகு பெறூஉ
மடிவாய்க் கோவலர் குடிவயிற் சேப்பி
னிருங்கிளை ஞெண்டின் சிறுபார்ப் பன்ன
பசுந்தினை மூரல் பாலொடும் பெறுகுவிர்
தொடுதோன் மரீஇய வடுவாழ் நோனடி
விழுத்தண் டூன்றிய மழுத்தின் வன்கை
யுறிக்கா ழூர்ந்த மறுப்படு மயிர்ச்சுவன்
மேம்பா டுரைத்த வோரி யோங்குமிசைக்
கோட்டவுங் கொடியவும் விரைஇக் காட்ட
பல்பூ மிடைந்த படலைக் கண்ணி
யொன்றம ருடுக்கைக் கூழா ரிடையன்

Perumbāṇaṟṟuppaḍai, 155–175.

[2] சுளை. [3] காய். [4] பாகல்.

[5] சேறு நாற்றமும் பலவின் சுளையும்
வேறுபடக் கவினிய தேமாங் கனியும்
பல்வே றுருவிற் காயும் பழனுங்
கொண்டல் வளர்ப்பக் கொடிவிடுபு கவினி
மென்பிணி யவிழ்ந்த குறுமுறி யடகு
மமிர்தியன் றன்ன தீஞ்சேற்றுக் கடிகையும்
புகழ்படப் பண்ணிய பேருன் சோறும்
கீழ்செல வீழ்ந்த கிழங்கொடு பிறவு
மின் சோறு தருநர்

Maduraikkāñji, 526–535.

[6] தான் ஞெலி தீ.

Puṛam, 150.

[7] யானை தந்த முளிமர விறகிற்
கானவர் பொத்திய ஞெலிதீ விளக்கு.

Ibid., 247.

kumpaṭṭi,[1] into which was poked a *śuḷundu*,[2] stalk sometimes tipped with sulphur.

Salt was manufactured on a large scale. Salt-fields have several names: *uppaḷam*,[3] *aḷakkar*,[4] *uvarkkaḷam*,[5] *uvaḷagam*,[6] *kaḻi*.[7] These names prove that salt-manufacture was an extensive industry, a fact which we could have inferred otherwise also, because the large use of vegetable food and especially of curries of innumerable kinds and of the many varieties of pickles to tempt the palate and satisfy its craving and to render rice and pulses tasty, requires the free use of salt.

The food of Northern and Southern India has remained unchanged for five thousand years and more. But the necessities of modern commerce have begun to alter it in many respects. Old ways of preparing foodstuffs and cooking them are giving way to new ones; the old methods of boiling and pounding paddy with the hand preserved the proteids and vitamins necessary for health and strength; but the new methods of hulling by machinery and polishing unboiled paddy are giving rise to the widespread diseases of civilization—tuberculosis and diabetes and to general enfeeblement. The old custom of eating leaf-curry and fruits cooked with their skins is giving way to modern refinements in cookery, and tinned provisions are taking the place of freshly made ones, so that the health of the people is steadily degenerating. The old forms of food were the result of thousands of years of experience, whereas the new ones, supposed to raise the standard of living, are really refined methods of committing slow suicide.

AGRICULTURE

Says Prof. G. Elliot Smith, 'I suppose most people would be prepared to admit that the invention of agriculture was the beginning of civilization. It involved a really settled society and the assurance of a food supply. Hence it created the two conditions without which there could have been no real development of arts and crafts and the customs of an organized form of society.'[8] Prof. Smith is of opinion that agriculture was developed in Egypt with the sowing of barley about ten thousand years ago and thence spread to other parts of the world. At about the same or perhaps a few millenniums earlier, as stone tools testify, the cultivation of paddy and the weaving of cotton began in the plains of South India. Hence the rise of Indian agriculture was not consequent on its development in Egypt.

Agriculture was the main industry of Ancient India, as it is to-day. It was carried on chiefly in the lower reaches of rivers where irrigation by means of canals is possible. Thus in the Śoḷa country, *Śoṇāḍu*,[9] the fertile delta of the Kāviri, even to-day the granary of South India and the island of Ceylon, was the main scene of agricultural operations. In the Pāṇḍya nāḍu, in the valleys of the Vaigai and the Tāmraparṇi wet cultivation was carried on. In the Śēra nāḍu which looked up to the sky for irrigation, the strip of coast west of the ghats where the rain it raineth every day during the monsoons, was devoted to this early industry of Indian man. In

[1] கும்பட்டி. [2] சுளுந்து. [3] [4] அளக்கர். [7] கழி.
[8] *Nature*, Jan. 15, 1927, p. 8. [9] சோணாடு.

other parts of the country there were small patches of Marudam, where rain-water straight from the sky, carried away by hill torrents, was stored and utilized for the raising of grains or vegetables. Where water supply was not on a generous scale, were raised grains and other crops which did not require a constantly wetted field to grow in. Hence cultivated land was divided into *nanśey*,[1] rice-growing field and *punśey*,[2] where other grains grow. Uncultivated land was *tariśu*.[3] *Śey*,[4] the common element of *nanśey*, and *punśey*, means a field as well as a particular area of land. It also means red and perhaps the word acquired the meaning of a field in the districts covered with red ferruginous clay. *Nanśey*, therefore, originally meant a good field and *punśey*, a bad field. Cultivated land was partitioned into fields. The field had numerous names : *vayal*,[5] *śey*, *agaṇi*,[6] *kambalai*,[7] *kaḻani*,[8] *kaidai*,[9] *kōṭṭam*,[10] *śeṟu*,[11] *taḍi*,[12] *paṇai*,[13] *paṇṇai*,[14] *paḻanam*,[15] *pānal*,[16] *pulam* ;[17] a small field was *kuṇḍil*,[18] *pātti*.[19] The large number of synonyms for *vayal*, was due to the fact that agriculture was the chief occupation of the people. Agriculture itself was called *vēḷāṇmai*,[20] the *āṇmai*,[21] lordship, of *vēḷ*,[22] land, *Vēḷaḷar*,[23] (a word different in origin from *veḷḷālar*)[24] were landowners, cultivators, *vēḷāṭṭi*,[25] being the feminine gender of the same. Owners of extensive tracts of land were called *vēḷ*, *veḷir* ; there were *kuṟunilamaṉar*, petty chiefs. After the Ārya social organization was imposed on Tamil India, *Vēḷāḷar* were given the name of *pūvaiśyar*, but the name has not stuck to them, for though they were technically Vaiśyas, the privileges of Vaiśyas were not really extended to them. *Vēḷāṇmai* was considered the noblest of occupations ; because the possession of grains conduces to the development of generosity. For, whereas other forms of wealth, especially minted metal, can be hoarded jealousy and will, if put out to interest, grow infinitely more and more, wealth in the form of food-grains will deteriorate if hoarded ; it will either be destroyed by vermin or will rot ; so the man who has a rich store will be naturally prompted to give it away to the poor and the starving. Hence India, the land of extensive agriculture, has become the land of unstinted charity ; hence *vēḷāṇmai* has become in Tamil synonymous with *īgai*,[26] (lit, gift), also *koḍai*.[27] The *Vēḷāḷar* were, by right of their instincts of charity, the nobles of the land and hence the characteristics of *vēḷāḷar*, *vēḷāṇmai māndar iyalbu*,[28] have been described as ten ; viz, (1) *āṇaivaḻi niṟṟal*,[29] keeping an oath, (2) *aḻindōrai niṟuttal*,[30] raising up the fallen, (3) *kaikkaḍanāṟṟal*,[31] being obliging, (4) *kaśivagattuṇmai*,[32] having compassion, (5) *ōkkalpōṟṟal*,[33] supporting relatives, (6) *ōvāmuyaṟchi*,[34] perseverance, (7) *manniṟaikaṟudal*[35] paying taxes, (8) *Oṟṟumaikōḍal*,[36] being peaceable, (9) *virundu*,[37] *puṟandarudal*, hospitality, (10) *tirundiyavoḻukkam*,[38] correct conduct. Of this list of virtues belonging to the Tamil farmer, *ōvāmuyaṟchi*, ceaseless toil, is the necessary result of rice-cultivation ; for more than other food-grains rice requires unceasing work

[1] நன்செய். [2] புன்செய். [3] தரிசு. [4] ெ [5] வயல். [6] அகணி [7] கம்பலை. [8] கழனி. [9] கைதை. [10] கோட்டம். [11] செறு. [12] தடி. [13] பணை. [14] பண்ணை. [15] பழனம். [16] பானல். [17] புலம். [18] குண்டில். [19] பாத்தி. [20] வேளாண்மை [21] ஆண்மை. [22] வேள். [23] வேளாளர். [24] வெள்ளாளர். [25] வேளாட்டி. [26] ஈகை. [27] கொடை. [28] வேளாண்மை மாந்தர் இயல்பு. [29] ஆணை வழி நிற்றல். [30] அழிந்தோரை நிறுத்தல். [31] கைக்கடனாற்றல். [32] கசிவகத்துண்மை. [33] ஒக்கல் போற்றல். [34] ஓவாமுயற்சி. [35] மன்னிறைகருதல். [36] ஒற்றுமைகோடல். [37] விருந்து புறந்தருதல். [38] திருந்தியவொழுக்கம்.

for several months in the year, patient endurance of the rheumatic pains, chills and other ills due to standing upto the knees in water and trudging on wet sticky clay ; this has made the Indian farmer a model of unfailing patience and enduring perseverance, and contributed to the development of what is miscalled fatalistic acceptance of misfortune. When the harvest was over and his granaries filled, he either gave himself up to the festivities of the post-harvest season, eating and drinking, singing and dancing, decorating his person with flowers and love-making developed as a fine art, or to martial exercises. In every village there was a field, *kaḷam*,[1] set apart for these purposes.[2] Another virtue of the farmer was his readiness to pay the king's taxes. All the world over, people are unwilling to pay taxes and many regard it almost as a virtue to evade payment of taxes. How is it then that the ancient Tamil landowner was differently constituted to modern men? The reason of this was the fact that taxes were payable in kind. A man with a well-filled granary easily parts with a portion of his abundance, all the more so because wealth in grains does not increase, but decreases with keeping ; but it is hard to part with specie, as it will keep all right for any length of time, and, if properly invested, barren metal will breed as fast as cattle and sheep, as Shylock well knew. Paying taxes in gold and silver is more difficult, especially if the purse is as ill-filled as generally the Indian farmer's purse is and if one has to borrow for paying taxes.

All the other virtues of the Veḷḷāḷar are but different forms of charity. It has already been explained how one who has a large store of cereals is easily induced to enjoy the pleasure of seeing his fellowmen feed on his substance. Numerous poetical names signifying *vēḷāḷar* exist. They are *maṇmagaḷ pudalvar*,[3] sons of the earth-goddess, *vaḷamaiyar*,[4] the flourishing, *kaḷamar*,[5] owners of fields, *maḷḷar*,[6] the strong, *kāvirippudalvar*,[7] sons of the Kāviri, *uḻavar*,[8] tillers, *mēḻiyar*,[9] ploughmen, *ērinvāḻnar*,[10] those that live by the plough, *iḷango*,[11] prince, *pinnavar*,[12] perhaps those that are behind *mannavar*,[13] *perukkāḷar*,[14] those that increase wealth, or those that utilize the food, *vinaiñar*,[15] toilers.

There was a wealth of vocabulary attached to each detail of agricultural operations. Ploughing was *uḻavu*,[16] *toyyil*;[17] hoeing, *kottudal*;[18] trampling, *uḻakkudal*,[19] *midittal*,[20] *maḍidal*;[21] manure,

[1] களம்.

[2] மன்னர் குழீஇய விழவி னானும்
மகளிர் தழீஇய துணங்கை யானும்
யாண்டுங் காணேன் மாண்டக் கோனை
யானுமோ ராடுகள மகளே என்கைக்
கோடீ ரிலங்கு வளை நெகிழ்த்த
பீடுகெழு குரிசிலுமோ ராடுகள மகனே

Kuṛundogai, 31.

I have searched for him in the places where heroes congregate (for martial exercises) ; and where women gather for the *tuṇaṅgai* but have not seen the magnificent hero ; hence I am but a woman of the theatre *āḍukaḷam* (ஆடுகளம்) ; the great hero too who has caused my bright bent bangles cut from conch shell to slip, is also a man of the theatre.

[3] மண்மகள்புதல்வர். [4] வளமையர். [5] களமர். [6] மள்ளர். [7] காவிரிப்புதல்வர். [8] உழவர். [9] மேழியர். [10] ஏரின்வாழ்நர். [11] இளங்கோ. [12] பின்னவர். [13] மன்னவர். [14] பெருக்காளர். [15] வினைஞர். [16] உழவு. [17] தொய்யில். [18] கொத்துதல். [19] உழக்குதல். [20] மிதித்தல். [21] மடிதல்.

eru,[1] *uram*.[2] *kuppai*,[3] *kūḷam*,[4] and so on. Different names were given for the fields other than that used for wet cultivation. A garden was *tōṭṭam*,[5] *tuḍavai*,[6] *paḍappai*,[7] *tōppu*,[8] *śōlai*,[9] *taṇḍalai*[10] (flower-garden), *kollai*,[11] (generally a kitchen-garden behind a house). High land was *tagar*,[12] *tarāy*,[13] *mēḍu*,[14] *ōngal*,[15] *karu*,[16] *kuppai*,[17] *kuvāl*,[18] *kuvai*,[19] *śuval*,[20] *tiḍar*,[21] *tiṭṭu*,[22] *tiṭṭai*,[23] *paḍar*,[24] *miśai*,[25] *vallai*,[26] *vanbāl*,[27] *murambu*:[28] this was so variously named, probably because it gave much trouble to the cultivator who had to level it before tilling it. The low land was also variously named, *paḷḷam*,[29] *aval*,[30] *iḻivu*,[31] *kiḻakku*,[32] *kīḻ*,[33] *kuḻi*,[34] *kūval*,[35] *ñeḷḷal*,[36] *tāḻvu*,[37] *paḍugar*,[38] *payambu*.[39]

The chief implement of the farmer was the plough; so he lovingly gave it numerous names, *kalappai*,[40] *idai*,[41] *uḻupaḍai*,[42] *kalanai*,[43] *ñāñjil*,[44] *toḍuppu*,[45] *paḍai*,[46] *paḍaivāḷ*.[47] The ploughshare was made of wood in the stone age and of steel in the iron age; both kinds are in use even to-day. The other important implement was the knife; it, too, had numerous names, *vāḷ*,[48] *uvaṇi*,[49] *ēdi*,[50] *kaḍuttalai*,[51] *tuvaṭṭi*,[52] *naviram*,[53] *nāṭṭam*,[54] *vañjam*,[55] *kuyal*,[56] *kuḷir*;[57] short knives were called *kuṟumbiḍi*,[58] *śurigai*,[59] one that could be bent into the handle, *śūri*.[60]

An extensive system of irrigation was practised; rivers were furnished with a complete dam, *aṇai*.[61] or a partial dam, *korambu*,[62] and the water diverted into a *kāl*,[63] *kālvāy*,[64] or *vāykkāl*.[65] Or water was raised from ponds or wells by means of an *ēṟṟam*[66] or *kabilai*[67] or *iṟaikūḍai*[68]. The latter was the most common means of raising water and had numerous names, *ambi*,[69] *iḍār*,[70] *iṟaivai*,[71] *kārāmbi*,[72] *kiḷār*,[73] *piḷār*,[74] *puṭṭil*,[75] *pūṭṭai*,[76] *paṭṭai*,[77] and conducted by means of a sluice, *maḍai*,[78] to higher levels and distributed to fields.

Here is a description of ploughing.—' The plough men, who raise food for many people, yoke trained oxen to the plough, whose front looks like the mouth of a female elephant, press it on the ground so that the ploughshare which looks like the face of the iguana, is buried in the earth. They plough round and round, then sow seeds and then weed the field. When the harvest season is near, the quail with short feet and black neck with its young, white and smelling like the

[1] எரு. [2] உரம். [3] குப்பை. [4] கூளம். [5] தோட்டம். [6] துடவை. [7] படப்பை [8] தோப்பு. [9] சோலை. [10] தண்டலை. [11] கொல்லை. [12] தகர். [13] தராய். [14] மேடு. [15] ஓங்கல். [16] கரு. [17] குப்பை. [18] குவால். [19] குவை. [20] சுவல். [21] திடர். [22] திட்டு. [23] திட்டை. [24] படர் [25] மிசை. [26] வல்லை. [27] வன்பால். [28] முரம்பு. [29] பள்ளம். [30] அவல். [31] இழிவு. [32] கிழக்கு. In the Kāviri valley which slopes from West to East *kīḻ* and *kiḻakku*, lit. lowland and *mēl*, *meṟku*, highland came to mean East and West respectively. [33] கீழ். [34] குழி. [35] கூவல். [36] ஞெள்ளல். [37] தாழ்வு [38] படுகர். [39] பயம்பு. [40] கலப்பை. [41] இதை. [42] உழுபடை. [43] கலனை. [44] ஞாஞ்சில். [45] தொடுப்பு [46] படை. [47] படைவாள் [48] வாள். [49] உவணி. [50] ஏதி. [51] கடுத்தலை. [52] துவட்டி. [53] நவிரம். [54] நாட்டம் [55] வஞ்சம். [56] குயல். [57] குளிர். [58] குறும்பிடி. [59] சுரிகை. [60] சூரி. [61] அணை. [62] கொரம்பு. [63] கால். [64] கால்வாய். [65] வாய்க்கால் [66] ஏற்றம். [67] கபிலை. [68] இறைகூடை. [69] அம்பி. [70] இடார். [71] இறைவை. [72] காராம்பி. [73] கிளார். [74] பிளார். [75] புட்டில். [76] பூட்டை. [77] பட்டை. [78] ம

Kadamba flower—*Eugenia racemosa*,—and unable to fly about, afraid of the noise of the harvesters, settles in the forest near.'[1]

Agriculture in South India was carried on exactly as it was in Āryāvartta. 'They ploughed the ground,[2] the plough being drawn by two oxen[3] fastened to the yoke with hempen or leather traces, and driven with a goad.[4] The ploughshare was made of iron[5] which supplanted the older ploughshare[6] made of Khadira wood. The ploughmen sang merrily to the steers while ploughing.[7] They bedewed the furrow with ghee and honey[8] before sowing. The fields were watered by means of irrigation canals from wells[9] or lakes, or by raising water from wells by means of wooden or metal buckets[10] tied to a rope, pulled round a stone pulley. They kept away birds from robbing them of the growing corn[11] by uttering loud cries.'[12]

Love in Marudam

The leisure enjoyed by agriculturists after the harvest was over led to the development of festivals among them, in which there was much singing, dancing and play-acting in order to pass idle moments. This again led to the growth of the institutions of harlotry, songstresses and actresses; *viraliar*[13] and *kūttiar*[14] were experts in the refinements of love. Numerous poems of the class Marudam deal with this subject. 'The festival is over. The drums are silent. Do you want to know what she thought then? I will tell you her thoughts. This young woman wore a leaf-garment; with that garment dangling on her lap, she walked along the streets. Then arose in the streets a great sound of laughter, as loud as when the followers of the great bowman Ōri, the victorious warrior-lord of Kolli, who was killed by Malaiyamān Tirumuḍikāri, saw Kāri enter the incomparably long streets of Ōri. On hearing that sound of laughter, the fair ladies who wore bangles and the skins of whose bodies was like the tender leaf of the mango, feared that she would capture the hearts of their

[1] குடிநிறை வல்சிச் செஞ்சா லுழவர்
நடைநவில் பெரும்பகடு புதவிற் பூட்டிப்
பிடிவா யன்ன மடிவாய் நாஞ்சில்
துடுப்பு முகமுழு முக்கொழு மூழ்கவூன்றித்
தொடுப்பெறிந் துழுத துளர்படு துடவை
யரிபுகு பொழுதி னிரியல் போகி
வண்ணக் கடம்பி னறுமல ரன்ன
வளரிளம் பிள்ளை தழீஇக் குறுங்காற்
கறையணற் குறும்பூழ் கட்சி சேக்கும்
வன்புலம்.

Perumbāṇāṟṟuppaḍai, 197–206.

[2] R. V. x. 101, 3; x. 106, 2.
[3] R. V. iii. 17, 3; x. 101, 3.
[4] A. V. iii. 25, 5; iv. 57, 4.
[5] A. V. iii. 17, 3.
[6] A V. v. 6, 6.
[7] A. V. viii. 20, 9.
[8] A. V. iii. 17, 9.
[9] A. V. i. 3, 7; iii. 13, 9; R. V. iii. 45, 3; vii. 49, 2, 4; x. 43, 7.
[10] R. V. x. 101, 5, 7.
[11] R. V. x. 68, 1.
[12] P. T. Srinivas Iyengar, *Life in Ancient India*, p. 23.
[13] விறலியர்.
[14] கூத்தியர்.

husbands and guarded them from her wiles. I have failed in these attempts, and she has seduced my lover away from me.'[1]

More innocent incidents of love also belong to *Marudam* ; such as the wailing of a wife when her husband has gone away to a far place after quarrelling with her. 'The sparrows whose wings are like the faded water-lily with petals shrunk and folded, and which reside in the roofs of houses, eat the paddy and the other grains spread for drying in the front yard of houses ; they make holes in the slender filaments of flowers in the highway. They return to their beds in the roof where they sleep with their young ones. Do not the sad evening and the pains of separation exist where he has gone.'[2]

PASTURAGE

As agriculture was the chief industry of *Marudam,* pasturage was the chief industry of *Mullai.* The sheep, the goat, the cow, the ox, the buffalo were the chief domestic animals tended by the *Āyar,* herdsmen. Profusion of names for each of these as usual indicates the love the herdsmen felt for their wards. Thus the sheep was called *āḍu,*[3] *uḍu,*[4] *oruvu,*[5] *turuvai,*[6] *tuḷḷal,*[7] *puruvai,*[8] *veṛi* ;[9] the red variety *śemmaṛi,*[10] *mōttai,*[11] *udaḷ,*[12] *ēḷagam,*[13] *paḷḷai,*[14] *kaḍā,*[15] *mai,*[16] *koṛi,*[17] *tagar,*[18] *meḻagam.*[19] The goat was called *veḷḷāḍu,*[20] *kārāḍu,*[21] *kochchai.*[22] *veḷḷai,*[23] *vaṛkāli* ;[24] *kuṛumbāḍu,*[25] from the wool of which *Kuṛumbar* wove *kamblies,* was also called *varuḍai,*[26] *varaiyāḍu.*[27] The cow had naturally the largest variety of names, *ā,*[28] *paśu,*[29] *kuram,*[30] *kurāl,*[31] *kūlam.*[32] *kovalam,*[33] *śurai* ;[34] a useless cow was *sudai* ;[35] a barren cow, *varchai,*[36] that which has yeaned once *kiṭṭi,*[37] *kiruṭṭi.*[38] The ox was *erudu,*[39] *iṛāl,*[40] *iṛu,*[41] *kuṇḍai,*[42] *kūḷi,*[43] *koṭṭiyam,*[44] *śe,*[45] *kō,*[46] *nūpam,*[47] *pagaḍu,*[48] *pāṇḍil,*[49] *pāṛal,*[50] *pullam,*[51]

[1] விழவு முழந்தன் றுமுழவுத் தூங்கின்
றெவன் குறித்தனன் கொலென்றி யாயிற்
றழை யணிந்தலமரு மல்குற் றெருவி
னிளையோ ளிறந்த வனைத்தற்குப் பழவிற்
லோரிக் கொன்ற வொருபெருந் தெருவிற்
காரி புக்க நேரார் புலம்போற்
கல்லென்றன்று ஊரே யதற்கொண்டு
காவல் செறிய மாட்டி யாய்தொடி
யெழின்மா மேனி மகளிர்
விழுமாந் தனர்தங்கொழுநரைக் காத்தே.

Naṛṛiṇai, 320.

[2] ஆம்பற் பூவின் சாம்ப லன்ன
கூம்பிய சிறகர் மனையுறை குரீஇ
முன்றி லுணங்கல் மாந்தி மன்றத்
தெருவி னுண்டாது குடைவன வாடி
யில்லிறைப் பள்ளித்தம் பிள்ளையொடு வதியும்
புன்கண் மாலையும் புலம்பு
மின்றுகொ றோழியவர் சென்ற நாட்டே.

Kuṛundagai, 46.

[3] ஆடு. [4] உடு. [5] ஒருவு. [6] துருவை. [7] துள்ளல். [8] புருவை. [9] வெறி. [10] செம்மறி. [11] மோத்தை. [12] உதள். [13] ஏழகம். [14] பள்ளை. [15] கடா. [16] மை. [17] கொறி. [18] தகர். [19] மேழகம். [20] வெள்ளாடு. [21] காராடு. [22] கொச்சை. [23] வெள்ளை. [24] வற்காலி. [25] குறும்பாடு. [26] வருடை. [27] வரையாடு. [28] ஆ. [29] பசு. [30] குரம். [31] குரால். [32] கூலம். [33] கோவலம். [34] சுரை. [35] சுதை. [36] வற்சை. [37] கிட்டி. [38] கிருட்டி. [39] எருது. [40] இறல். [41] இறு. [42] குண்டை. [43] கூளி. [44] கோட்டியம். [45] சே. [46] கோ. In view of the fact that *kōn* was a pure Tamil word for a cowherd, I regard *kō* as independent of Sanskrit *go* the resemblance between the words being absolutely accidental. [47] நூபம். [48] பகடு. [49] பாண்டில். [50] பாறல். [51] புல்லம்.

pūṇi,[1] *peṟṟam*,[2] *pōttu*,[3] *mūri*,[4] *viḍai*.[5] Of these names *kāḷi*[6] means breeding bull; those which were used by traders for bearing burden, (*podi*)[7] were called *tūriyam*,[8] *pagaḍu*,[9] and *pāṟal*.[10] The buffalo was called *kavari*,[11] *kārā*,[12] *kārām*,[13] *mūri*,[14] *mēdi*;[15] *vaḍavai*,[16] barren ones, *maimai*;[17] the bull calf of the buffalo, *kuḻavi*,[18] *kanṟu*.[19] Its cow-calf *ā*,[20] *nāgu*;[21] the bull-buffalo, *umbal*,[22] *ēṟu*,[23] *oruttal*,[24] *pagaḍu*,[25] *pōttu*.[26] The udder of the cow and of the buffalo, *maḍi*,[27] *śeruttal*;[28] *māḍu*[29] was the general name of both the cow and the buffalo. Intimate acquaintance with animals developed a great love of them and the invention of a number of words relating to them. Thus beasts in general were called *vilangu*,[30] *kurangam*,[31] *mā*,[32] *mān*;[33] their young ones, *kuruḷai*,[34] *kuṭṭi*,[35] *piḷḷai*,[36] *maṟi*,[37] *kanṟu*,[38] *kuḻavi*,[39] *pārppu*,[40] *magavu*.[41] Hornless animals were called *kumaram*;[42] the horn was *ulavai*,[43] *kōḍu*,[44] *maruppu*;[45] the tail, *tōgai*,[46] *kūlam*,[47] *vēśagam*.[48]

Tame Animals

The tame animals that were of use to man were *mān*,[49] deer, also named *uḻai*,[50] *ēnam*,[51] *śūnam*,[52] *navvi*,[53] *piṇaimari*;[54] its male, *iralai*,[55] *ēṟu*,[56] *oruttal*,[57] *karumān*,[58] *kalai*,[59] *pulvāy*;[60] its female, *piṇai*;[61] its young, *ēṇi*,[62] *kanṟu*,[63] *kuḻavi*,[64] *tannam*,[65] *paṟam*,[66] *pārppu*,[67] *maṟi*.[68] The ass *kaḻudai*,[69] besides the bullock, was a burden-bearer. The horse, *kudirai*,[70] was not a native of South India, and was imported in later times from Sind and Persia. The pig, *panṟi*,[71] was another useful animal and was also named *ari*,[72] *iruḷi*,[73] *eṟuḻi*,[74] *ēnam*,[75] *karumā*,[76] *kaḷiṟu*,[77] *kānal*,[78] *kānmā*,[79] *kiḍi*,[80] *kiri*,[81] *kēḻal*,[82] *kōṭṭuma*,[83] *maimmā*,[84] *mōḻal*.[85]

The dog first tamed by the hunter and then trained by the keeper of the cattle to watch the fold, was named, *nāy*,[86] *akkan*,[87] *aśuḻam*,[88] *aṟpam*,[89] *eginam*,[90] *kukkan*,[91] *kūran*,[92] *śuṇangan*,[93] *ñamali*,[94] *ñāḷi*,[95] *tuttam*,[96] *pāsi*;[97] its female, *pāṭṭi*,[98] *piṇai*,[99] *muḍuval*;[100] the pup, *kuṭṭi*,[101] *kuruḷai*,[102] *pāṟal*;[103] the cat was called *alavan*,[104] *indi*,[105] *ōdi*,[106] *pavanam*,[107] *pākkan*,[108] *pilli*,[109] *pūsai*,[110] *pūñai*,[111] *verugu*;[112] it was also poetically called, *iṟpuli*,[113] the house-tiger; the male cat was specially named *kaḍuvan*,[114] *pōttu*;[115] the kitten, *kuṭṭi*,[116] *pāṟal*,[117] *piḷḷai*.[118]

1 பூணி. 2 பெற்றம். 3 போத்து. 4 மூரி. 5 விடை. 6 காளி. 7 பொதி. 8 தூரியம். 9 பகடு. 10 பாறல். 11 கவரி. 12 காரா. 13 காரான். 14 மூரி. 15 மேதி. 16 வடவை. 17 மைமை. 18 குழவி. 19 கன்று. 20 ஆ. 21 நாகு. 22 உம்பல். 23 ஏறு. 24 ஒருத்தல் 25 பகடு. 26 போத்து. 27 மடி. 28 செருத்தல். 29 மாடு. 30 விலங்கு. 31 குரங்கம். 32 மா 33 மான். 34 குருளை. 35 குட்டி. 36 பிள்ளை. 37 மறி. 38 கன்று 39 குழவி. 40 பார்ப்பு. 41 மகவு. 42 குமரம். 43 உலவை. 44 கோடு. 45 மருப்பு. 46 தோகை. 47 கூலம் 48 வேசகம். 49 மான். 50 உழை. 51 ஏனம். 52 சூனம். 53 நவ்வி. 54 பிணைமரி. 55 இரலை. 56 ஏறு. 57 ஒருத்தல். 58 கருமான். 59 கலை 60 புல்வாய். 61 பிணை. 62 ஏணி. 63 கன்று. 64 குழவி. 65 தன்னம். 66 பறம். 67 பார்ப்பு. 68 மறி. 69 கழுதை. 70 குதிரை. 71 பன்றி. 72 அரி. 73 இருளி. 74 எறுழி 75 ஏனம். 76 கருமா. 77 களிறு. 78 கானல். 79 கான்மா. 80 கிடி. 81 கிரி. 82 கேழல். 83 கோட்டுமா. 84 மைம்மா. 85 மோழல். 86 நாய். 87 அக்கன். 88 அசுழம். 89 அற்பம். 90 எகினம். 91 குக்கன். 92 கூரன். 93 சுணங்கன். 94 ஞமலி. 95 ஞாளி. 96 துத்தம். 97 பாசி. 98 பாட்டி. 99 பிணை. 100 முடுவல். 101 குட்டி. 102 குருளை. 103 பாறல். 104 அலவன். 105 இந்தி. 106 ஓதி. 107 பவனம். 108 பாக்கன். 109 பில்லி. 110 பூசை. 111 பூஞை. 112 வெருகு. 113 இற்புலி 114 கடுவன். 115 போத்து. 116 குட்டி. 117 பாறல். 118 பிள்ளை.

The other beasts familiar to the people were *aṇil*,[1] the squirrel; *karaḍi*,[2] the bear, *kāṭṭā*,[3] the wild cow, *kīri*,[4] the mongoose, *kuraṅgu*,[5] the monkey, *nari*,[6] the jakal, *śennāi*,[7] the wild dog, the *nāy*,[8] or the *kōnāy*,[9] the wolf, *nīrnāy*,[10] the beaver, *nāvippiḷḷai*,[11] the civet cat, *muṭpaṉṟi*,[12] the porcupine, *maraimān*,[13] the yak, *muśu*,[14] the ape, *muyal*,[15] the hare, *yānai*,[16] the elephant.

The chief house-pests were *eli* [17] the rat, *kāreli*, [18] the black rat, *peruchchāḷi*,[19] the bandicoot, *mūnjūṟu*, [20] the mouse and the ubiquitous mosquito, *kośu*,[21] which was such a great nuisance as to receive a dozen other names, *aśaval*,[22] *añalam*,[23] *ulaṅgu*,[24] *śagal*,[25] *tummu*,[26] *tuḷḷal*,[27] *nilambi*,[28] *nulumbu*,[29] *noḷḷal*,[30] *muñal*,[31] *valu*,[32] *añal*;[33] *ī*,[34] the house-fly and *andu*,[35] insect found in stored grain. But the bed bug seems to be an import from abroad, for, it has but a *kāraṇappeyar*, i.e. *mūttaippūcchi*,[36] the bundle-insect.

Birds

There are many general names for birds *paṟavai*,[37] *kuḍiñai*,[38] *kurugu*,[39] *puḷ*;[40] their young ones, *kuñju*,[41] *pārppu*;[42] the cry of birds *payir*;[43] their nest, *kaṭchi*,[44] *kuñjuṟai*,[45] *kuḍambai*,[46] *kurambai*,[47] *kūṇḍu*.[48] A flock of birds was called *tholudi*,[49] the cries of a flock, *tuḷani*;[50] the beating of a birds' wings, *ośanaittal*,[51] *puḍaittal*;[52] female birds are called *peḍai*,[53] *peṭṭai*,[54] *pēḍai*;[55] the females of birds other than the gallinaceous fowl and the owl, *aḷagu*;[56] their males except in the case of the peafowl and the *eḻāl*,[57] *śēval*;[58] the cock of the peafowl and the *eḻāl*, *pōttu*.[59] The food of birds and of some animals *irai*,[60] *uṇḍi*,[61] *uṟai*,[62] *ūṭṭi*.[63]

The following are names of some species of birds:—*anṟil*,[64] nightingale, *annam*,[65] swan *āndai*,[66] large eyed owl, *uḷḷān*,[67] snipe, *ūrkkuruvi*,[68] sparrow, *tūkkaṇāṅguruvi*,[69] *kavudāri*,[70] partridge, *kavudam*,[71] king-fisher, *kaḻugu*,[72] eagle, *kākkai*,[73] crow, *nīrkkākkai*,[74] a diving water-bird, *kāḍai*,[75] quail, *kiḷi*,[76] parrot, *kuyil*,[77] cuckoo, *kurugu*,[78] village fowl, also *kōḻi*,[79] another variety, *kūgai*,[80] large hooting owl, *kokku*,[81] stork, *śādagam*,[82] sky-lark, *śichchili*,[83] king-fisher, *sival*,[84] *pagaṇḍai*[85], another species of partridge, *sembōttu*,[86] *nārai*,[87] heron, *parundu*,[88] kite, *purā*,[89] pigeon, *mayil*,[90] peafowl.

The love of nature and close observation of natural objects which was a great characteristic of the Tamils of ancient times are constantly revealed in early Tamil poems. On later Tamil Poetry the conventions of the later artificial Sanskrit Poetry wielded

1 அணில். 2 கரடி. 3 காட்டா. 4 கீரி. 5 குரங்கு. 6 நரி. 7 செந்நாய். 8 நாய். 9 கோநாய். 10 நீர்நாய். 11 நாவிப்பிள்ளை. 12 முட்பன்றி. 13 மரைமான். 14 முசு. 15 முயல். 16 யானை. 17 எலி. 18 பெருச்சாளி. 19 காரெலி. 20 மூஞ்சூறு. 21 கொசு. 22 அசவல். 23 அஞலம். 24 உலங்கு. 25 சகல். 26 தும்மு. 27 துள்ளல். 28 நிலம்பி. 29 நுளம்பு. 30 நொள்ளல். 31 முஞல். 32 வலு. 33 அஞல். 34 ஈ. 35 அந்து. 36 மூட்டைப்பூச்சி 37 பறவை. 38 குடிஞை. 39 குருகு. 40 புள். 41 குஞ்சு 42 பார்ப்பு. 43 பயிர். 44 கட்சி. 45 குஞ்சுறை 46 குடம்பை. 47 குரம்பை. 48 கூண்டு. 49 தொழுதி. 50 துழனி. 51 ஓசனைத்தல். 52 புடைத்தல். 53 பெடை. 54 பெட்டை 55 பேடை. 56 அளகு. 57 எழால். 58 சேவல். 59 போத்து 60 இரை. 61 உண்டி. 62 உறை. 63 ஊட்டி. 64 அன்றில். 65 அன்னம் 66 ஆந்தை. 67 உள்ளான். 68 ஊர்க்குருவி. 69 தூக்கணாங்குருவி. 70 கவுதாரி. 71 கவுதம். 72 கழுகு. 73 காக்கை. 74 நீர்க்காக்கை. 75 காடை. 76 கிளி. 77 குயில். 78 குருகு 79 கோழி. 80 [illegible] 81 கொக்கு. 82 சாதகம். 83 சிச்சிலி 84 சிவல் 85 பகண்டை. 86 செம்போத்து. 87 நாரை. 88 பருந்து. 89 புறா. 90 மயில்.

great influence. Not so on the natural poetry of the earlier ages. To illustrate the keen observation of Fauna on the part of the poets, a few quotations are given. 'The pods of the Phaseolus mungo are like the red legs of the quail.'[1] 'The leaf of the *Caladium nymphæfolium* which grows on the hill, rich and waving, moved by the cold northwind in the month of Tai, resembles the ears of the elephant'.[2] 'The water-lily growing in deep pools resembles the back of the yellow-legged crane'[3] The carp, afraid that the stork would eat it, ducked under the water, but found itself near the lotus and equally feared its bud.'[4] 'The nightingale which dwells on the palmyra leaves cries gently.'[5] 'In the cold weather the *Cassia* flower like ourselves gets golden dots and the twig of the memecylon *tinctorium* is filled with flowers and looks like the neck of a peacock.'[6] 'The path traced by the claws of the crab will be extirpated by the waves of the sea.'[7] 'The mountain from which honey-combs are hanging, as (the trappings from) the chariot.'[8] 'The goat has a belly like the false skin of the flowering bean.'[9] 'The flock of yellow legged fish-eating storks look like the pearls on the breast of Murugan when they fly in the red sky.'[10] 'The shaggy head of the ñemai tree looks like the rows of flags on the royal elephant. The spiders' webs round the tree waved in the west wind that blew over the hill called Ōḍai; the lean elephants mistook them for clouds and lifted their trunks to catch them and sounded like the *tūmbu*[11] of the actors.'[12]

[1] பூழ்க்காலன்ன செங்காலுழுந்து. *Kuṛundogai*, 68.

[2] சிலம்பிற் சேம்பினலங்கல் வள்ளிலை
பெருங்களிற்றுச் செவியின் மானத்தைஇத்
தண்வரல் வாடை தூங்கும்
கடும்பனி. *Ib*. 76.

[3] பைங்காற் கொக்கின் புன்புறத்தன்ன
குண்டுநீ ராம்பல். *Ib*. 122.

[4] குருகுகொளக் குளித்த கெண்டை யயல
துருகெழு தாமரை வான்முகை வெரூஉம். *Ib* 127.

[5] மன்றலம் பெண்ணை மடல்சேர் வாழ்க்கை
யன்றிலும் பையென நரலும். *Ib*. 177.

[6] கொன்றையம் பசுவீ
நம்போற பசக்குங் காலை
... ...காயாம் பூக்கெழு பெருஞ்சினை
மென்மயி லெருத்திற் றோன்றும். *Ib*. 183.

[7] அலவன் கூருகிர் வரித்த
வீர்மணல் வீர்நெறி சிதைய விழுமென
வுருமிசைப் புணரி. *Ib*. 351.

[8] நிரைசேர் நுண்டேர் போலப்
பிரசந் தூங்குமலை. *Ib*. 392.

[9] பூங்கொடி யவரைப் பொய்யதள் அன்ன
வுள்ளில் வயிற்ற வெள்ளை வெண்மறி.
Agam 104.

[10] நெடுவேள் மார்பினாரம் போலச்
செவ்வாய் வானத்தீண்டி மீனருந்தும்
பைங்காற் கொக்கினிரை பறை யுகப்ப. *Ib*. 120.

[11] யானைக் கொண்டதுகிற் கொடிபோல
வலந்தலை ஞெமையத்து வலந்த சிலம்பி
யோடைக் குன்றத்துக் கோடையொடு துயல்வர
மழையென மருண்ட மம்மர் பலவுடன்
ஞெய்களி றெடுத்த நோயுடை நெடுங்கை
தொகுசொற் கோடியர் தூம்பினுயிர்க்கும். *Ib*. 111.

[12] தூம்பு. a musical instrument.

'Green parrot with the red bill, who go on picking the bent stalks of the panicum, do not fear me; give up the fear that any one would threaten you for picking the stalks. When you have finished with them and are at leisure, attend to my wants; I join my palms and beg you to help me in this affair. If you go to your relatives who live in my lover's country, where grows the jack tree which bears abundant fruits, meet my lover who is the lord of this mountain and tell him that the young *Kuṛava* woman of the forest around this mountain is guarding the millet field to-day as usual.'[1]

'The banyan tree bears many boughs full of fruits; to eat the fruit many birds crowd round the tree. Their cries resemble the sound of many musical instruments.'[2]

'The crowds of beets which have thin wings eat the honey, and after the honey is exhausted desert the flowers.[3]

'The *āral*,[5] lamprey, with nose like an ear of corn, creeps into the mud; the *vāḷai*,[6] *Trichiurus lepturus*, which has a horn, moves tremulously on the water; the fishermen approach the tank which have flowers bright as the flame, the tortoise looks like the hollow-bowelled *kiṇai*,[7] (the drum of the *marudam*); the gravid *varāl*,[8] *Ophicephalus striatus*, is like the *nugumbu*[9] of the palmyra; with it fights the *kayal*,[10] carp, which shines like a spear.'

Trees and Plants

The ancient Tamils distinguished and named innumerable trees, plants, shrubs and creepers and knew their properties. The pure Tamil names of a few trees alone will be here referred to: *achcham*,[11] *Coronilla grandiflora*, commonly called *agatti*,[12] probably after Agastiya, *atti*,[13] Indian fig, *anichchai*,[14] a sensitive tree, *āchchā*,[15] *Diospyros ebenaster*, *ātti*,[16] *Bauhineara cemosa*, *āl*,[17] the banyan, *itti*,[18] *Ficus virens*, *ilandai*,[19] jujube, *ilavam*,[20] the silk-cotton tree, *iluppai*,[21] the long-leaved Bassia, *īndu*,[22] *Phoenix farinifera*, *usil*,[23] *Acacia pennata*, *eṭṭi*,[24]

[1] கொடுங்குரல் குறைத்த செவ்வாய்ப் பைங்கிளி
யஞ்ச லோம்பி யார்பதங் கொண்டு
நின்குறை முடித்த பின்றை யென்குறை
செய்தல் வேண்டுமால் கைதொழு திரப்பல்
பல்கோட் பலவின் சாரலவர் நாட்டு
நின்கிளை மருங்கிற் சேறி யாயி
னம்மலை கிழவோற் குரைமதி யிம்மலைக்
கானக் குறவர் மடமக
ளேனல் காவ லாயின ளெனவே. *Naṛṛiṇai*, 102.

[2] கோளிபல முரஞ்சிய கோளி யாலத்துக்
கூடியத் தன்ன குரல்புணர் புள். *Malaipaḍukaḍām*, 268–269.

[3] நுண்டா தூண்டி வறும்பூத் துறக்கு
மென்சிறை வண்டினம். *Maduraikkāñji*, 573.

[4] கதிர்மூக் காரல் கீழ்ச்சேற் றொளிப்பக்
கணைக்கோட்டு வாளை மீநீர்ப் பிறழ
வெரிப்பூம் பழன நெரித்துடன் வலைஞ
ரரிக்குட ரரியின் யாமை மிளிரப்
பனைநுகும் பன்ன சினைமுதிர் வராலொ
டெறிவே லன்ன வொண் கயல்.

Puṛam, 249.

[5] ஆரல். [6] வாளை. [7] கிணை. [8] வரால். [9] நுகும்பு, perhaps the tender kernel of the fruit.
[11] அச்சம். [12] அகத்தி. [13] அத்தி. [14] அனிச்சை. [15] ஆச்சா. [16] ஆத்தி
[18] இத்தி. [19] இலந்தை. [20] இலவம். [21] இலுப்பை. [22] ஈந்து. [23] உசில். [24] எட்டி.

Strychnos nux vomica, *elumichchai*,[1] the lemon tree, *ōmai*,[2] the mango, also *mā*,[3] *kadambu*,[4] *Eugenia racemosa*, *kaḍavu*,[5] *Gyrocarpus jacquini*, *kaḍu*,[6] the gall-nut tree, *kamugu*,[7] the areca palm, *karuṅgāli*,[8] the ebony, *kaḷḷi*,[9] *Euphorbia tirucalli*, *kāya*,[10] *Memecylon tinctorium*, *kurundu*,[11] *konṛai*,[12] Cassia, *śandanam*,[13] or *āram*,[14] sandal-wood tree, *teṅgu*,[15] cocoanut tree, *tēkku*,[16] teak, *nāval*,[17] the jambolan tree, *nelli*,[18] Indian gooseberry, *palā*,[19] the jack tree, *panai*,[20] palmyra, *pādiri*,[21] *Bignonia chelonoides*, *pālai*,[22] the iron-wood tree, *puḷi*,[23] the tamarind tree, *punnai*,[24] the Alexandrian laurel, *pūvaraśu*,[25] the Portia tree, *pūvandi*,[26] the soapnut tree, *magiḻ*,[27] a tree of very sweet smelling flower, *mādaḷai*,[28] the pomegranate, *muruṅgai*,[29] *Hyperanthera murunga*, *mūṅgil*,[30] the bamboo, *vāgai*,[31] *marudam*,[32] *Terminalia alata*, *vanni*,[33] *Prosopis spicigera*, *vilvam*,[34] *Crataeva religiosa*, *viḷā*,[35] the wood-apple, *vēṅgai*,[36] the *Pterocarpes bilobus* *vembu*,[37] the margosa tree. The names of smaller plants, and of different kinds of leaves and flowers are so numerous that it is not possible to catalogue them or even to mention the more familiar varieties. The unblown flower was called *arumbu*,[38] the parts of flowers, *idaḻ*; [39] *pūndēn*; [40] young trees *nāgu*; [41] fruiting trees, *palinam*,[42] trees with heart-wood inside, *āṇmaram*,[43] with heart-wood outside, *peṇmaram*,[44] branch, groups of trees without heart-wood, *ali*,[45] *veḷiṟu*,[46]; the synonyms of the word, tree, are very considerable in number. I will content myself with noting a few poetic images which show how keen was the observation of nature by the ancient Tamils :—

'The gourd (*pīrkku*,[47]) with round, white flowers grows along with the thin creeper *muśuṇḍai*,[48] on shrubs.' [49]

'The hill country has bamboos which wave to and fro and its clear clouds spread the dew amidst the peacocks whose expanded tails shine like the sapphire.' [50]

'The forest land possesses the expanding jasmine, *taḷavu*,[51] the broad November flower, *tōnṟi*,[52] the mullai with the petals opened, the *tēru*,[53] (clarifying-nut tree) which drops its flowers, the *konṟai*,[54] Cassia, whose flowers are like gold, the *kāyā*,[55] whose flowers are like sapphire.' [56]

'The *kuravam*,[57] has flowered; the cold weather is gone; in the beautiful spring, in the river, a slender stream is running; the wide river with straight stretches of sand has its banks adorned with many

1 எலுமிச்சை. 2 ஓமை. 3 மா. 4 கடம்பு. 5 கடவு. 6 கடு. 7 கமுகு. 8 கருங்காலி. 9 கள்ளி, 10 காயா. 11 குருந்து 12 கொன்றை. 13 சந்தனம். 14 ஆரம். 15 தெங்கு. 16 தேக்கு. 17 நாவல். 18 நெல்லி. 19 பலா. 20 பனை. 21 பாதிரி. 22 பாலை. 23 புளி. 24 புன்னை. 25 பூவரசு. 26 பூவந்தி. 27 மகிழ். 28 மாதளை. 29 முருங்கை. 30 மூங்கில். 31 வாகை. 32 மருதம். 33 வன்னி. 34 வில்வம். 35 விளா. 36 வேங்கை. 37 வேம்பு. 38 அரும்பு. 39 இதழ். 40 பூந்தேன். 41 நாகு. 42 பலினம். 43 ஆண்மரம். 44 பெண்மரம். 45 அலி. 46 வெளிறு. 47 பீர்க்கு. 48 முசுண்டை. *Iponœa Candicans*.

49 புன்கொடி முசுண்டைப் பொறிப்புற வான்பூப்
பொன்போற் பீர்மொடு புதற்புதல. *Neḍunalvāḍai*, 13–14.

50 மணி மயிற் கலாப மஞ்சிடைப் பரப்பித்
துணிமழை தவழும் துயல்கழை நெடுங் கோடு.

Śiṟupāṇāṟṟuppaḍai, 264–5.

51 தளவு. 52 தோன்றி. 53 தேறு. 54 கொன்றை. 55 காயா.

56 அவிழ்தளவி னகன்றோன்றி
நகுமுல்லை யுகுதேறுவீப்
பொற்கொன்றை மணிக்காயா.

Porunarāṟṟupaḍai, 199–201.

57 குரவம்.

marudam trees; the mango has its branches decorated with tender leaves; the smoke-like cloud creeps along its boughs filled with bunches of flowers; the cuckoos enjoy the beauty of the scene and sing.'[1]

'The roots of the bamboo are intertwined with each other; when the winds blow upon them they sound like the sigh of the elephant tied to its post. Looking at the moon which crept over the hill standing in a forest of bamboos, I said to myself, another moon (his mistress with a face bright as a moon) with teeth sharp as thorns and a fair face adorned by a sweet-smelling mark (*tilakam*) is standing on the hills, on whose rocks grow trees whose bare branches have shed their leaves in the strong gale, did I not?'[2]

'The *konṛai* flowers spread on a pit cut in a stone resemble a box of the wealthy man, filled with gold coins and kept open.'[3] 'The cool flowers of the *tāḻai* (screw-pine), which has bent thorns, when scattered by the winds, run like the pearls of a garland when the thread is snapped, on the white sands of the sea-shore.'[4]

'The garden was crowded with tall bamboos from which thorns hang and on which rest the cuckoos, which have bent claws and thin blue feathers, after drinking the mango juice, sweet as if milk were mixed with it, and after that, the sour juice of the *nelli* fruit.'[5]

'The *mullai*, jasmine, which flowers in places adjoining a stream looks like the teeth of a cat laughing.'[6]

1 குரவுமலர்க்
தற்சிர ந்கிய வரும்பவிழ் வெளி
லறலவிர் வார்மண லகவியாற் றடைகரைத்
துறையணி மருதமொ டிகல்கொள வோங்கிக்
கலுழ்தளி ரணிந்த விருஞ்சினை மாஅத்
திணர்தகை புதுப்பூ நிரைத்த பொங்கர்ப்
புகைபுரை யம்மஞ் சூர
நுகர் குயிலகவும்.

Agam, 97.

2 வேர்பிணி வெதிரத்து [illegible]
கந்துபிணி யானை யயர்வுயிர்த் தன்ன
வென்றூழ் நீடிய வேய்பிறங் கழுவத்துக்
குன்றூர் மதியை நோக்கி நின்று நினைந்
துள்ளினெ னல்லனோ யானே முள்ளெயிற்றுத்
திலகம் தைஇய தேங்கமழ் திருநுத
லெமது முண்டோர் மதிநாட் டிங்க
ளுரறுகுரல் வெவ்வளி யெடுப்ப நிழற்பல
வுலவை யாகிய மரத்த
கல்பிறங்கு மாமலை யும்பரஃ தெனவே.

Naṛṛiṇai, 62.

3 கவலை கெண்டிய கல்வாய்ச் சிறுகுழி
கொன்றை யொள்வீ தா ஆய்ச்செல்வர்.
பொன்பெய் பேழை மூய்திறந் தன்ன.

Kuṛundogai, 233.

4 கூன்முண் முண்டகக் கூர்ம்பனி மாமலர்
நூலறு முத்திற் காலொடு பாறித்
துறைதொறும் பறிக்குந் தூமணல்.

Ib., 51.

5 பால்கலப் பன்ன தேக்கொக் கருந்துபு
நீல மென்சிறை வள்ளுகிர்ப் பறவை
நெல்லியம்புளி மாந்தி யயலது
முள்ளி லம்பணை மூங்கிலிற் றூங்குங்
கழைநிவந் தோங்கிய சோலை. *Ib.*, 201.

6 அருவிசேர் மருங்கிற் பூத்த முல்லை
வெருகுசிரித் தன்ன. *Ib.*, 220.

Ideal of Feminine Beaut

A people so acutely observant of natural objects and capable of keen relish of their beauty would naturally deal largely in descriptions of feminine charms; of numerous references to this subject I shall quote but one :—The songstress had hair like the black sand on the sea-shore; her fair forehead was like the crescent moon, her eye-brow bent like the bow that kills; the outer end of her cool eyes was beautiful, her sweetly speaking mouth was red like the sheath of the fruit of the silk cotton tree; her spotlessly white teeth were like rows of many pearls; her ears were like the curved handles of scissors and their lobes were shaking with bright ear rings shaped like the crocodile. Her neck was bent down with modesty; her shoulders were like the waving bamboo trees; her forearms were covered with thin hair; her fingers were like the November flower which grows on the tops of high hills; her brightly shining nails, like the mouth of a parrot. Her breasts, covered with light coloured beauty spots, were such as people thought that it would cause her pain to bear them, and were so high that the rib of a cocoanut leaf could not go between them; her navel was very beautiful and resembled a whirl-pool in water. Her waist was so small that observers could not guess that it existed (and that it bore the weight of the body) with difficulty. Her pudendum was adorned with a *mēgalai*, many stringed waist band with many bells, looking as if it swarmed with bees; her thighs, straight and thin like the trunk of a female elephant; her lower legs were covered with hair, as it ought to be, up to the ankles, and her small feet were like the tongue of a tired dog.[1]

Industries

Carpentry began and was well developed in the Stone Age; for all sorts of carpenter's tools have been picked up from the settlements of the lithic epoch. Most of these tools were made of iron when the Iron Age succeeded. The workers in wood was called *tachchar*[2] or *yāṇar*.[3] Carpenters had a greater variety of work to do than in modern days, for besides making the wooden furniture and utensils in

[1] அறல்போற் கூந்தற் பிறைபோற் றிருநுதற்
கொலைவிற் புருவத்துக் கொழுங்கடை மழைக்க
ணிலவிதழ் புரையு மின்மொழித் துவர்வாய்ப்
பலவுறு முத்திற் பழிதீர் வெண்பன்
மயிர்குறை கருவி மாண்கடை யன்ன
பூங்குழை யூசற் பொறைசால் காதி
னாணடச் சாய்ந்த நலங்கிள ரெருத்தி
னாடமைப் பணைத்தோ ளரிமயிர் முன்கை
நெடுவரை மிசைஇய காந்தண் மெல்விரற்
கிளிவா யொப்பி னொளிவிடு வள்ளுகி
ரணங்கென வுருத்த சுணங்கணி யாகத்
தீர்க்கிடைப் போகா வேரிள வனமுலை
நீர்ப்பெயர்ச் சுழியி னிறைந்த கொப்பூ
ழுண்டென வுணரா வுயவு நடுவின்
வண்டிருப் பன்ன பல்கா ழல்கு
லிரும்பிடித் தடக்கையிற் செறிந்துதிரள் குறங்கிற்
பொருந்துமயி ரொழுகிய திருந்துதாட் கொப்ப
வருந்து நாய் நாவிற் பெருந்தகு சீறடி. *Pornāuṟṟuppaḍai*, 25-47.

[2] தச்சர். [3] யாணர்.

household use, they had also to build houses, palaces, and temples, carts and chariots. Turning and wood-carving were highly developed. The legs of sitting planks and swinging planks were turned according different designs. Every available corner of wooden articles in houses, carts, and chariots were filled with wood carving, of elaborate patterns carved in minute detail with the extraordinary patience that the Indian artist alone is capable of. No work, big or small, left the carpenter's hands without some art work on it so that there was no sharp distinction as there is in Europe between utilitarian and artistic work. So much so that one of the synonyms for *tachchan*[1] is *śittiran*,[2] artist.

Boat building was also an ancient form of wood-work, but was in the hands of men who lived in *Neydal*, that is, coast land. It is worth noting that the boat builders were affiliated with fishermen, so far as social status was concerned. The work of the boat-builder is no less skilful than that of other carpenters ; but yet the social position of the later was much higher than that of the former. This was partly because the boat-builders shared in the food and the personal habits of the fishermen among whom they lived ; moreover the wood-work of the boat builder is cruder than that of the carpenter and does not admit of art work like other forms of wood work, so that the boat-builder had the status of the journeyman worker whereas the carpenters were allotted the privileges of the artist. While the boat-builders were of low status, chariot-makers were the companions of kings.

Workers in metal were called *kammāḷar*,[3] *akkasālaiyar*,[4] *aṟivar*,[5] *ōvar*,[6] *kaṇṇāḷar*,[7] *kaṇvinaiñar*,[8] *kammiyar*,[9] *kollar*,[10] *karumār*,[11] *taṭṭār*,[12] *tuvaṭṭar*,[13] *pulavar*,[14] *punaiyar*,[15] *vittagar*,[16] *vittiar*,[17] *vinaiñar*.[18] They worked in iron, steel, copper, bronze, silver and gold. They were very skilful workers as is proved by the specimens of jewels and utensils recovered from ancient graves. Huge vessels of these various metals were made by hammering into shape immense blocks of metals. This requires much more skill than the method of cutting out sheets, *adar*,[19] *tagadu*,[20] of metal, bending them into the shapes of the different parts of a vessel and rivetting or soldering them together, such as is done now. The import of large sheets of thin metal from Germany has made our workers forget the art of hammering out big vessels and making them without joints. The delicate carving on gold and silver that was the glory of ancient India is not yet dead, thanks to the love of personal decoration which modern civilization has not yet been able to root out of the souls of our ladies. Ladies loved jewels so much that there are many words which mean 'to wear jewels,' e.g., *aṇi*,[21] *ār*,[22] *śūḍu*,[23] *punai*,[24] *pūṇ*,[25] *malai*,[26] *milai*,[27] *milai*,[28] *vēy*,[29] *ey*,[30] *vey* ;[31] the noun forms of many of these words mean jewels. Some professions subsidiary to that of the goldsmiths 'who heat good gold and make shining jewels out of it'[32]

1 தச்சன். 2 சித்திரன் 3 கம்மாளர். 4 அக்கசாலையர் 5 அறிவர் 6 ஓவர். 7 கண்ணாளர். 8 கண்வினைஞர். 9 கம்மியர். 10 கொல்லர். 11 கருமார். 12 தட்டார். 13 துவட்டர். 14 புலவர். 15 புனையர். 16 வித்தகர். 17 வித்தியர். 18 வினைஞர். 19 அடர். 20 தகடு. 21 அணி. 22 ஆர். 23 சூடு. 24 புனை 25 பூண். 26 மலை. 27 மிலை. 28 மிலை. 29 வேய். 30 எய். 31 வெய்.

32 சுடுநன் பொன் சுடரிழை புனைநரும். *Maduraikkāñji*, 512.

were those of the *kaḍainar*,[1] who 'turn cut conch shells into bangles,[2] *kuyinar*,[3] 'who drill holes in beautiful gems'[4].

The weaver's art was equally well developed. They were called *kammiyar*,[5] *śēṇiyar*,[6] *kārugar*.[7] They hawked clothes about in the streets of towns. 'Young and old weavers assembled where four streets met, stood with their legs touching each other and spread clothes whose folds, short and long, resembled the waves of the sea.[8]

Similes derived from the work of these workmen are found in literature. One such runs as follows:—'The legs of the crab are like the open jaws of the smith who works at the furnace where air is blown in by pressing bellows made of soft skin.'[9] 'The leaves of the water-lily are caught in the thorny rasplike stem of the cane which grows on the edges of ponds and waves slowly in the unsteady north-wind and swells and swings like the bellows which drive air quickly into the furnace of the smith.'[10] 'The male bear which has a wide mouth, seeking food, breaks an ant hill whose surface is covered by curved lines and its grunt frightens the snakes which reside in the ant-hill; then it sighs like the nose of the furnace where the smith heats iron.'[11]

Here is a splendid simile derived from the work of the blacksmith:—

'His chest was as hard as the anvil which stands before the furnace lighted in the smithy where the blacksmith with strong arms turns iron into implements that may be used against the enemy.'[12]

2 கோடுபோழ் கடைநரும்

Maduraikkāñji, 511.

3 குயினர். 4 திருமணி குயினரும்.

Ib., 511.

5 கம்மியர். 6 சேணியர். 7 காருகர்.

8 தெண்டிரை யவிரறல் கடுப்ப வொண்பல்
குறியவு நெடியவு மடிதரூஉ விரித்துச்
சிறியரும் பெரியருங் கம்மியர் குழீஇ
நால்வேறு தெருவினுங் காலுற நிற்றர.

Ib., 519–522.

9 மென்றோன்
மிதியுலைக் கொல்லன் முறிகொடிற் றன்ன
கவைத்தா ளலவன்.

Perumbāṇāṟṟupaḍai, 206-8.

10 பொய்கை யடைகரைப் பிரம்பி
னாரவா ரன்ன வம்மு ளைநெடுங்கொடி
யருவி யாம்ப லகலடை துடக்கி
யசைவரல் வாடை தூக்கலி னூதுலை
யிசைவாங்கு தோலின் வீங்குபு நெகிழும்.

Agam, 96.

11 இரைதே ரெண்கின் பகுவா யேற்றை
கொடுவரிப் புற்றம் வாய்ப்ப வாங்கி
நல்லரா நடுங்க வுரறிக் கொல்ல
னூதுலைக் குருகி னுள்ளுயிர்த்து.

Naṟṟiṇai, 125.

12 பகைவர்க்
கிரும்பு பயன்படுக்குங் கருங்கைக் கொல்லன்
விசைத்தெறி கூடமொடு பொரூஉ
முலைக்க லன்ன வல்லா ளன்னே.

Puṟam, 170.

Other professions that deserve mention are that of the toddy-drawer, oil presser, sugar-cane presser, manufacturer of jaggery and of liquor.

TRADE

The word for trade *vaṇigam*[1] is usually supposed to be derived from Sanskrit *vāṇijyam*. The probabilities are just the other way about. *Vaṇiyam* is derived from *vaṇik* or *baṇik*, merchant, and this later word is almost certainly from the vedic *paṇi*. The *paṇis* were the traders of Vedic times and as they were Dasyus and would not pay *dakshiṇā* to the performers of Ārya rites the Rishis denounced them as being niggards.[2] The *paṇis* being Dasyus were most probably the Tamil traders of the early Vedic epoch, for in those days the Tamils alone of South Indians were the most civilized tribes and the objects of internal trade, then and for long after, were, as it has been already pointed out, South Indian products like pearls, corals, sandal wood, pepper, and other spices. Hence the word *paṇi* and its variants and derivatives must have passed to North India from the South; hence Tamil *vaṇiga* became *baṇik* and *paṇi*. There is a Vedic root *paṇ*, to negotiate, which in later Sanskrit came to mean to stake. This root may have been coined from *paṇi*.

Trade first began in Neydal. For the *paradavar*[3] of that region, where cereals could not be raised, could get only fish and salt to eat. Now it may be possible to keep up life solely on fish, all the courses from soup to pudding being made from that one food-stuff, but one cannot live comfortably for any length of time on fish alone, notwithstanding the fact that the remote ancestors of all animals were aquatic beings; for very soon the hankering for vegetable food will assert itself. So the ancient dwellers of the littoral tracts learnt to carry fish and salt and (later salted fish) to the neighbouring *marudam* and barter their goods for cereals. Hence in the poems belonging to the *Neydal tiṇai*[4] there is frequent mention of the trade in salt. One instance of it may be given. 'His wounds caused by the sword-fish having been cured, my father has gone to the big blue sea for fishing; my mother too has gone to the salt fields to barter salt for white rice; so if the lover comes now he can without any hindrance meet his mistress.'[5]

Sellers of salt were called *umaṇar*,[6] *umaṭṭiyar*.[7] This ancient trade in which a double bag of salt was placed like a saddle on the back of a bull, which was driven from place to place in the interior of the land, can be observed even to-day in far-off villages. When the salt trade reached greater proportions it was carried in carts. 'The wheel, *uruḷi*[8] of the cart was surrounded by a round rim *śuṭṭu*[9] which went round the spokes, *ār*,[10] tightly fixed to the hub *kuṛadu*,[11] which looked like a drum, *muḻavu*.[12] The strong yoke, *pār*,[13] was fastened to two long beams placed on the axle-tree, *parūkkai*,[14] which looked like an *eḻū*,[15] timber placed between two elephants to prevent them from fighting with each other. Its top, *vāy*,[16] bore a creaking mat of *ragi* stalks, *ārvai*,[17] as the hill bears clouds on its top. In the

[1] வணிகம். [2] R. V. vi. 51. 14; vii. 22. 6. [3] பரதவர். [4] நெய்தல்திணை.

[5] சுரு வெறிந்த புண்டணிந் தெந்தையு
நீனிறப் பெருங்கடல் புக்கனன் யாயு
முப்பை மாறி வெண்ணெற் றரீஇய
வுப்புவிளை கழனி சென்றன ளதனாற்
பனியிரும் பரப்பிற் சேர்ப்பற்
கினிவரி னெளியள். *Kuṛundogai*, 269.

[6] உமணர் [7] உமட்டியர். [8] உருளி. [9] சுட்டு. [10] ஆர். [2] முழவு.
[13] பார். [14] பருக்கை. [15] எழு. [16] வா [17] ஆர்வை.

front of a hut which possessed a hen-coop, resembling a loft from which men guard the crops from being devasted by elephants, was a woman, with a child at her side, and a twig of margosa with flowers and leaves held in her hands to protect the child from demons ; she stood near the yoke from which was hanging a pot of vinegar, tied with strings like the drum of a dancing girl on a dancing platform ; and she beat the back of the bull with a wooden mortar whose mouth was as big as the knee of a female elephant with tusks resembling the shoot of a bamboo. Their men who wore garlands of flowers and leaves, whose shoulders were big, beautiful and strong, and whose limbs were supple and powerful, walked by the cart to whose yokes rows of bulls were tied with ropes passing through small holes ; the men saw that the carts were not upset. They fixed the price of salt in terms of other articles and passed along the road with teams of reserve bulls to replace those that became exhausted.'[1]

What an extremely realistic and at the same time highly poetical description of a subject which no modern man would regard as capable of poetic treatment at all !

Another article hawked about from place to place was pepper. Grown in Malabar, the land of the Śēras, it was a necessary ingredient of curry throughout South India. 'Pepper bags looking like the small-pulped big jack fruit which grows at the foot of the majestic jack-tree are balanced on the strong, scarred, prick-eared donkey which carries the pepper along long roads where tolls are collected. These roads are guarded by bow-men.'[2]

Gradually as cities grew in size, the power of monarchs grew to ample proportions, civilization advanced, and trade in numerous articles of necessity and luxury grew in the land. In cities 'there were people who vended various things including many beautiful looking

1. கொழுஞ்சூட் டருந்திய திருந்துநிலை யாரத்து
முழவி னன்ன முழுமர வுருளி
யெழூஉப் புணர்ந்தன்ன பருஉக்கவை நோன்பார்
மாரிக் குன்ற மழைசுமந் தன்ன
வாரை வேய்ந்த வறைவாய்ச் சகடம்
வேழங் காவலர் குரம்பை யேய்ப்பக்
கோழி சேக்குங் கூடுடைப் புதவின்
முன்னேயிற திரும்பிடி முழந்தா ளேய்க்குந்
துளையரைச் சீறா றூங்கத் தூக்கி
நாடக மகளி ராடுகளத் தெடுத்த
விசிவீங் கின்னியங் கடுப்பக் கயிறுபிணித்துக்
காடி வைத்த கலனுடை மூக்கின்
மகவுடை மகடூஉப் பகடுபுறந் தரப்பக்
கோட்டிணர் வேம்பி னேட்டிலை மிடைந்த
படலைக் கண்ணிப் பரேரெறுழ்த் திணிதோள்
முடலை யாக்கை முழுவலி மாக்கள்
சிறுதுளைக் கொடுநுக நெறிபட நிரைத்த
பெருங்கயிற் றொழுகை மருங்கிற் காப்பச்
சில்பத வுணவின் கொள்ளை சாற்றிப்
பல்லெருத் துமணர் பதிபோகு நெடுநெறி

Perumbāṇāṟṟuppaḍai, 46–65.

2. தடவுநிலைப் பலவின் முழுமுதற் கொண்ட
சிறுசுளைப் பெரும்பழங் கடுப்ப மிரியல்
புணர்ப்பொறை தாங்கிய வடுவாழ் நோன்புறத்
தணர்ச்செவிக் கழுதைச் சாத்தொடு வழங்கும்
உல்குடைப் பெருவழிக் கவலைக் காக்கும்
வில்லுடை வைப்பு.

ibid., 77–82.

articles of food, produced in the hill country, in the low country and in the sea. There were traders who, brought different kinds of brilliant gems, pearls and gold from far off lands.... There were men who assayed gold; there were sellers of clothes, vendors of copper vessels which were sold by weight, men who, when their business was over, tied the proceeds to their loin cloth, men who sold choice flowers, and scented pastes. There were clever painters, *kaṇṇuḷ vinaiñar*,[1] who painted pictures of all kinds of minute incidents'.[2] This description pertains to the trade of the beginning of the first millennium A.D., but this trade could not have differed from that of a very much earlier epoch, because civilization did not grow by leaps and bounds in any particular period, but grew so gradually that the life conditions of any one epoch resembled very much those of previous ages.

'Traders carried jewels to foreign countries on ships that had sails spread in the wind and that sailed on the ocean whose waves smelt of fish'.[3] They carried jewels for sale on land, but in a country where the *Maṛavar* followed as their only profession that of highway robbery, the travels of traders were fraught with adventure. 'The merchants who enabled all men to enjoy the grand things which are found on the mountain and in the sea have breasts full of scars made by the piercing arrows, clothes tied tight round their waists and a knife stuck into it, strong broad shoulders to which was attached the cruel bow and so resembled *Murugan* who wears the *Kaḍambu* flower. They held in their hands a big spear like *Yaman*. A stinging dagger with a white handle made of ivory, looking like a snake creeping on a hill, was tied with a belt to their shoulders; their strong feet were covered with shoes and they wore coats'.[4]

[1] கண்ணுள் வினைஞர்.

[2] பல்வேறு பண்டமோ டூண்மலிந்து கவினி
மலையவு நிலத்தவு நீரவும் பிறவும்
பல்வேறு திருமணி முத்தமொடு பொன்கொண்டு
சிறந்த தேஎத்துப் பண்ணியம் பகர்நரும்
... ...
பொன்னுரை காண்மருங் கலிங்கம் பகர்நருஞ்
செம்புநிறை கொண்மரும் வம்புநிறை முடிநரும்
பூவும் புகையு மாயு மாக்களு
மெவ்வகைச் செய்தியு முவமங்காட்டி
நுண்ணிதி னுணர்ந்த நுழைந்த நோக்கிற்
கண்ணுள் வினைஞரும். *Maduraikkānji*, 503-6, 513-18.

'பண்ணியம்' in this passage meaning an article of trade is a derivative of *Paṇi* trader.

[3] வாலிதை யெடுத்த வளிதரு வங்கம்
... ...
நனந்தலை வினைஞர் கலங்கொண்டு மறுக. *Ib.*, 536 and 539.

[4] மலையவுங் கடலவு மாண்பயந் தரூஉ
மரும்பொரு ளருந்தத் திருந்துதொடை நோன்று
யடிபுதை யரண மெய்திப் படம்புக்குப்
பொருகணை தொலைச்சிய புண்டீர் மார்பின்
விரவுவரிக் கச்சின் வெண்கை யொள்வாள்
வரையூர் பாம்பின் பூண்டுபுடை தூங்கச்
சுரிகை நுழைந்த சுற்றுவீங்கு செறிவுடைக்
கருவி லோச்சிய கண்ணக னெறுழ்த்தோட்
கடம்பமர் நெடுவே ளன்ன மீளி
யுடம்பிடித் தடக்கை யோடா வம்பலர். *Perunbānāṛṛuppaḍai*, 67-76.

Balances for weighing articles of trade were of two kinds. One was the steel-yard called *ñemankōl*[1] or *niraikōl*;[2] this was made of wood and resembled the steelyards used in villages to-day; rich merchants, however, used steelyards made of ivory.[3] The second was the *tarāśu*,[4] a pair of scales. All this trade was carried on by barter, as old Indians did not like to coin metal, and when they got coins from foreign countries, made jewels of them for their bosoms or hoarded them deep in the bosom of mother-earth.

Traders, in the Tamil country, were and are called *śeṭṭi*.[5] This word has been sanskritized into *śreshṭhī* and assimilated to the adjective *śreshṭha*, excellent. *Śreshṭī* is by some supposed to have degenerated into *śeṭṭi*; I consider this derivation to be a topsy-turvy one. *Śeṭṭi* is the personal noun from *śeṭṭu*, trade, a *śeṭṭi* being one who pursues *śeṭṭu*, trade, as his profession; for it is absurd to think that the Tamil traders carried on their profession for ages without a name for their profession or for themselves as followers of the profession. Hence it is reasonable to infer that *śreshthi* is Tamil *śeṭṭi* dressed in a Sanskrit garb. Sanskrit scholars suffer from a form of superiority-complex and believe that Sanskrit, the language of the Gods, being a perfect language, could not stoop so low as to borrow words from the languages of men. Hence they are fond of inventing derivations, ingenious and plausible, but absurd from a historical point of view, for words borrowed from foreign sources. Thus they say that *hammīra*, borrowed from Persian *amīr*, is a contraction of *aham vīrah*; they explain *kshatrapa*, satrap also borrowed from Persian, as *kshtram pātīti kshatrapah*; they derive *horā*, which was borrowed from Greek, from *ahorātram*, with its head and its tail amputated. The derivation of *śeṭṭi* from *śreshthī* is of a piece with these products of a perverse ingenuity.

The capital with which the ancient traders traded was called *mudal*,[6] initial stock. I wonder whether *mudaliyār*[7] meant originally men with *mudal*. There has always been a rivalry between *mudaliar* and *piḷḷai*[8] with regard to social status; does this point to an ancient rivalry between merchants and agriculturists? We have no materials which can help us to solve this question. Literary evidence merely indicates that both those who produced crops and those who sold them belonged to the class of *mēlōr*,[9] who were qualified to become the heroes of love poems.

Trade on any scale would scarcely be possible without debts. The word *kaḍan*[10] shows that debts were contracted in olden times. Interest was called *vaṭṭi*,[11] a word usually identified with prakrit *vaḍḍi* Sanskrit *vriddhi*. The Tamil word might as well be derived from Tamil *vaṭṭu*, a small piece, or *vaṭṭi*, cowries, cowries being small change, *sillaṛai*.[12] *Vāśi*[13] meant a deduction other than *vāṭṭi*; the literal meaning of the word seems to be 'additional'. The places where mercantile transactions took place were *kaḍai*,[14] *maḷigai*,[15] *aṅgāḍi*,[16] and *sandai*,[17] which has become in English 'Shandy'.

[1] நெமன்கோல். [2] நிறைகோ[illegible]

[3] யானை வான்மருப் பெறிந்த வெண்கடை
கோனிறைத் துலாஅம். *Puṛam* 39.

[4] தராசு. [5] செட்டி. [6] முதல். [7] முதலியா[illegible] [8] பிள்ளை. [9] [illegible] [10] [illegible]
[11] வட்டி. [12] சில்லறை. [13] வாசி. [14] கடை [15] மளிகை. [16] [illegible] [17] [illegible]சந்தை.

There are several minor subjects about which the evidence of pure Tamil words and of early literature can be profitably used, but which I have now no time to deal with. Those subjects are: Diseases and medicines, knowledge of human and animal anatomy, notions of jurisprudence, recognized terms of relationship, death-rites, division of time, astronomical notions, knowledge of colours. of meteorological phenomena, reading and writing, notions of psychology and ethics. Without the inclusion of these subjects, our reconstruction of the life of the ancient Tamils will not be complete.

This life of the Tamil people slowly evolved from the beginning of the Old Stone Age, that of the Āryas of North India began to influence. This was not a catastrophic inroad into the south from the north but a very slow process of infiltration. This infiltration began in the middle of the third millennum B.C. Then Paraśurāma settled with a number of followers, south of the Vindhyas. Many of Viśvamitra's sons, soon after, migrated to South India, as the *Aitareya Brāhmaṇa* informs us. But yet at the beginning of the second millennium B.C., when Rāma crossed the Godāvarī, the non-Aryan Rākshasas were predominant in Southern India and the southernmost Ārya colony was that of the Āgastyas on the banks of that river. In the age of the Mahābhārata, in which Tamil soldiers took part, Ārya influence in Southern India increased. But still in about the sixth century B.C. Āpastambha, the last of the Sūtrakāras, called a Rishi by courtesy, flourished near the banks of the Godāvarī and made laws for the Āryas there. Tamil India produced no Rishi, neither a Rishi of the *mantradrashṭā* type, nor even of the later type of the promulgator of the Śrauta, Gṛihya, and Dharma Sūtras. Into the Tamil land, Brāhmanas, Bauddhas, and Jainas spread in the centuries preceding and succeeding the beginning of the Christian era. The early Pallavas of Kāñchī were chiefly responsible for this migration of the Āryas. Notwithstanding the widespread of Brāhmaṇas, literature was chiefly in the hands of the Tamil *Pāṇar* and hence neither the Sanskrit language nor Sanskrit literature exercised much influence till about the fifth century after Christ. Early in that age, Tṛiṇadhumāgni, author of *Tolkāppiyam*, tried to adapt the social system of the northerners to the Tamil people, but without any success. Meanwhile the religious ideas of the *Itihāsas* spread among the common people. The teachings and practices of the Bauddhas and the Jainas were also promulgated from the monasteries of those monks. The complicated rites of Siva-worship and Vishṇu-worship as propounded in the Āgamas were adopted by the people and temple rites became the monopoly of a special sect of Brāhmaṇas; as a result of this, these two cults became wedded to the Ārya system of four varṇas, ill-adjusted to the old scheme of Tamil classes. One of the results of this was the extension of the idea of endogamous caste and the rise of innumerable castes marked by endogamy—an idea unknown to the Tamils of the early ages. Another result was that Tamil lost its linguistic and literary independence. A copious flow of Sanskrit words into the Tamil tongue took place. In the region of literature, the old ode, *agaval*[1] gave place to *kāviyam*.[2] Not only literary forms but also literary images, literary conventions, and poetic images, belonging to

[1] அகவல்

Sanskrit, crept into Tamil poems. The *Mokshaśāstram* of the northerners, reprezented by the *Upanişhads*, the *Bhagavad Gītā* and the *Vedānta Sūtras*, prevailed in the South. Very soon South India more than amply repaid this debt to North India by producing the three great *Bhāshyakāras*—Śaṅkara, Rāmānuja and Ānandatīrtha.

The genius of Tamil is marked by the scientific temperament; concrete ideas and images appeal to the Tamil people and hence Tamil is peculiarly fitted to be the vehicle of scientific knowledge. The genius of Sanskrit is marked by the philosophical temperament; it revels in abstractions which are the life-breath of philosophy. It was the wedding of Tamil genius and Sanskrit genius that is responsible for South Indian thinkers having become the guides of Indian thought during the last thousand years. In our days the genius of Europe has begun to influence India. The great ambition of Europe is to amass wealth and to utilize it for raising the standard of life, by developing the means of attainment of the ever-increasing methods of appealing to the senses, not only the five senses, but also that of locomotion. How far the genius of Europe is going to alter the life of the Tamils is concealed in the womb of time. We have succeeded in tearing the veil of past time and getting a few glimpses of ancient life; but future time is covered by a veil of nebulous matter which cannot be pierced by any known methods of enquiry.